WATERSHEDDINGS MEMORIES 1889—1997

Without the assistance of advertisers this book would not be possible.

To each of them, many thanks!

Thank you to Melvyn Lord, Reddish Demolition Ltd., for sponsoring the book.

WATERSHEDDINGS MEMORIES 1889—1997

The Oldham Rugby League Heritage Trust

Steve Brown - Mick Harrop
Michael Turner - Brian Walker

The earliest known photograph of Oldham at Watersheddings circa 1897 / 8.
(See also page 33 for another image from this match.)

Players identified in the casual team group include: Arthur Lees, Joe Lawton, Emanuel Bonser, Herbert Ellis, George Frater and R.L. (Dicky) Thomas.

ISBN 978-0-9546393-4-1

Printed and bound by:
Vertical Editions, Skipton, North Yorkshire.

THE OLDHAM RUGBY LEAGUE HERITAGE TRUST:

The Trust was formed by a group of Oldham RLFC supporters who first met back in 1995 to discuss the formation of the Oldham RLFC Hall of Fame.

At that time it was realised that in and around the town there were a number of people who owned representative caps, medals and other awards won by Oldham players from bygone eras, some of whom wished to donate those items to the Hall of Fame.

To protect the ownership of this collection and at the same time ensure it was kept available for generations of Oldham people to come, the Trust, under the guidance of OMBC Museum, the Charity Commission and a local firm of solicitors, was formed.

Many of the items in the collection have been donated but from time to time the Trust bids for Oldham rugby league - related items at auction, again in an attempt to either keep them in the borough, or bring them back to the town.

As a result of the Trust's endeavours the people of Oldham now have access to one of the finest rugby club collections of important memorabilia in the world and it's still growing!

Exhibitions - a record attendance for OMBC's flagship "Gallery Oldham" - when its collection was displayed there. A permanent Oldham RLFC showcase is sited in the Rugby League Heritage Centre at the George Hotel, Huddersfield – the birthplace of rugby league.

Film shows - rugby enthusiasts attended the sell-out showing of the Mitchell & Kenyon collection of Edwardian rugby films in conjunction with the British Film Institute.

Books – *Watersheddings' Memories* is the fourth from the Trust's presses and the fifth surrounding the 'Roughyeds'.

Should you visit the Trust's website www.orl-heritagetrust.org.uk besides uncovering a mine of information surrounding the Oldham club's rich history and its players, you will find details of many books and publications that have connections with the club.

© Oldham Rugby League Heritage Trust: 2010

Oldham Chairman Jim Quinn (centre), seen here with Hall Of Fame members (left to right) Bernard Ganley, Alan Davies, Bob Irving, Alex Givvons (who officially opened the Hall Of Fame) and Andy Goodway.

1st November 1995.

Thanks to everyone who has contributed photographs, news-clippings and other images used within this book.

Some may not be of the finest quality but nevertheless priceless when portraying the events that make up the history of a fine old stadium like Watersheddings, one of the most famous grounds in the rugby playing world.

ACKNOWLEDGEMENTS:

We would like to give special thanks to the following individuals who have been most helpful in the preparation of this book:

Geoff Cooke, Ian Wilson, Tom Wadsworth, Donald Walton, Joyce Pilkington, Robert Gate, Trevor Simms, Mr. Power, Brian Holland, John Blair, Sean Baggaley (social history curator - Gallery Oldham), Andy Yates, Eddie Whitham, Harry Edgar (Rugby League Journal), Tim Hughes, John Beever (G.S. Designs), Andrew Varley, Sam Kershaw, Trevor Jones, Keith Shaw, Barrie Gallagher, Jennifer Turner, Arthur Brown, Dave Whitehead, Graham Richmond, Jude Lawrence, Andy Wilson, John Etty, Mike Ford, Roger Halstead, Ray Hicks, Frank Stirrup, Ray French, Martin Murphy, John Donovan, Ian Clayton, Peter Young, Sid Little, Janice & Des McKeown, Jim Rochford and Terry Flanagan.

Also the late Tony Davies and Jean Brooks.

The Oldham Evening Chronicle
The Oldham Local Studies Library

Cover design: Sarah Turner.

INTRODUCTION

The first game played at the appropriately named but much loved Watersheddings, perched in the Pennine hills, wasn't rugby as you might have expected but cricket. It was a match played on the stadium's cricket field on the 14th of June 1889 between Oldham Cricket Club and Nelson Cricket Club. Nelson won.

The first rugby match – in those days subject to the rules of the Rugby Football Union - was played on the 28th of September between Oldham Football Club and Swinton, although it is believed that a trial match against local rivals Crompton had been played on the previous Wednesday.

To the west of the new stadium the skyline was dominated by the cotton spinning Ruby Mill, which was constructed during the same year as the stadium, a fact proudly borne out by its massive chimney which had emblazoned into its brickwork RUBY 1889. Cotton was king, the town was booming and those who were developing the fledgling multi-sports stadium had every right to feel optimistic.

Oldham Football Club (later to become Oldham Rugby League Football Club) went financially from strength to strength, reflected by their success on the field, but in 1911, twenty two years after their move to Watersheddings, the cricket club found themselves in financial disarray and forced to disband. The rugby club, sub-tenants of the cricket club, took over the lease allowing the cricket club to reform paying a nominal rent. In 1922 the stadium was bought outright by the rugby club for £4,375.

The earlier history of the two clubs was intertwined. The cricket club, founded after a meeting held at the Black Swan Hotel at Bottom O' th' Moor in 1852, first played on a piece of land rented from Lord Stamford at Hollinhall, before moving the short distance down the hill from Greenacres to Clarksfield. Founded in 1876, Oldham FC, with its headquarters at the very same Black Swan Hotel, played for the first two seasons of its existence on a piece of land on Glodwick Lows sited just behind the mill owned by Glodwick Spinning Company, but unable to accommodate paying spectators, moved into Clarksfield as sub-tenants of the cricket club.

Both clubs eventually outgrew Clarksfield, where play had been hampered by the slope. On the 1st of January 1889 the cricket club negotiated a lease on a piece of farmland up at Watersheddings, whilst the rugby club looked to play on land close to the Woodstock Mill at Royton Junction. This fell through, so once again the rugby club became the sub-tenant of the cricket club, this time at Watersheddings.

Following a lucrative offer to the rugby club from a greyhound racing syndicate the cricket club, founder members of the Central Lancashire League, moved to the old Borough Ground situated at the end of the nearby Broadbent Rd. Opened ceremoniously in 1934 by their president and former mayor of Oldham, Frank Pollard, the ground was renamed in his honour. They still play there - slap bang in the middle of Watersheddings Village – while in recent years the rugby league club has led a nomadic existence.

The successful playing period during the fifties allowed not just the adjacent land to be acquired, to be used primarily as a training pitch, but a state-of-the-art scoreboard to be erected and a new stand built behind the posts at the Watersheddings end of the ground. In 1965 floodlights were erected and finally, in 1967, the social club was opened.

But, by the mid eighties, the financial status of the club had spiralled downwards and severe new ground safety regulations forced the Herbert St. side seating areas to be demolished, signalling the beginning of the end for Watersheddings.

In the summer of 1997 the stadium was demolished.

Down the years international, county, schoolboy, amateur and professional rugby, county and club cricket, greyhound racing, baseball, both men's and women's soccer, bowls, boxing, wrestling and tennis had featured there, as had jubilee celebrations, military parades, pageants, maypole dancing, police dog training and even pram races. Some of the concerts held in the old social club became legendary!

But, first and foremost Watersheddings was

famous for being the home of Oldham Rugby League Football Club and for over a century was graced by the most famous players of the sport. Thousands of us, some of us scattered to the four corners of the earth, will each cherish our own memories of Watersheddings, whether it might be a packed to the rafters thrill-a-minute Tuesday night Challenge Cup replay or queuing at half-time at a second team match for a plastic cup of luke-warm coffee in the driving rain. By using a collection of hundreds of enthralling photographs, documents, newspaper clippings and other images – many published for the first time and others not seen for more than a hundred years all but the ghosts are remembered.

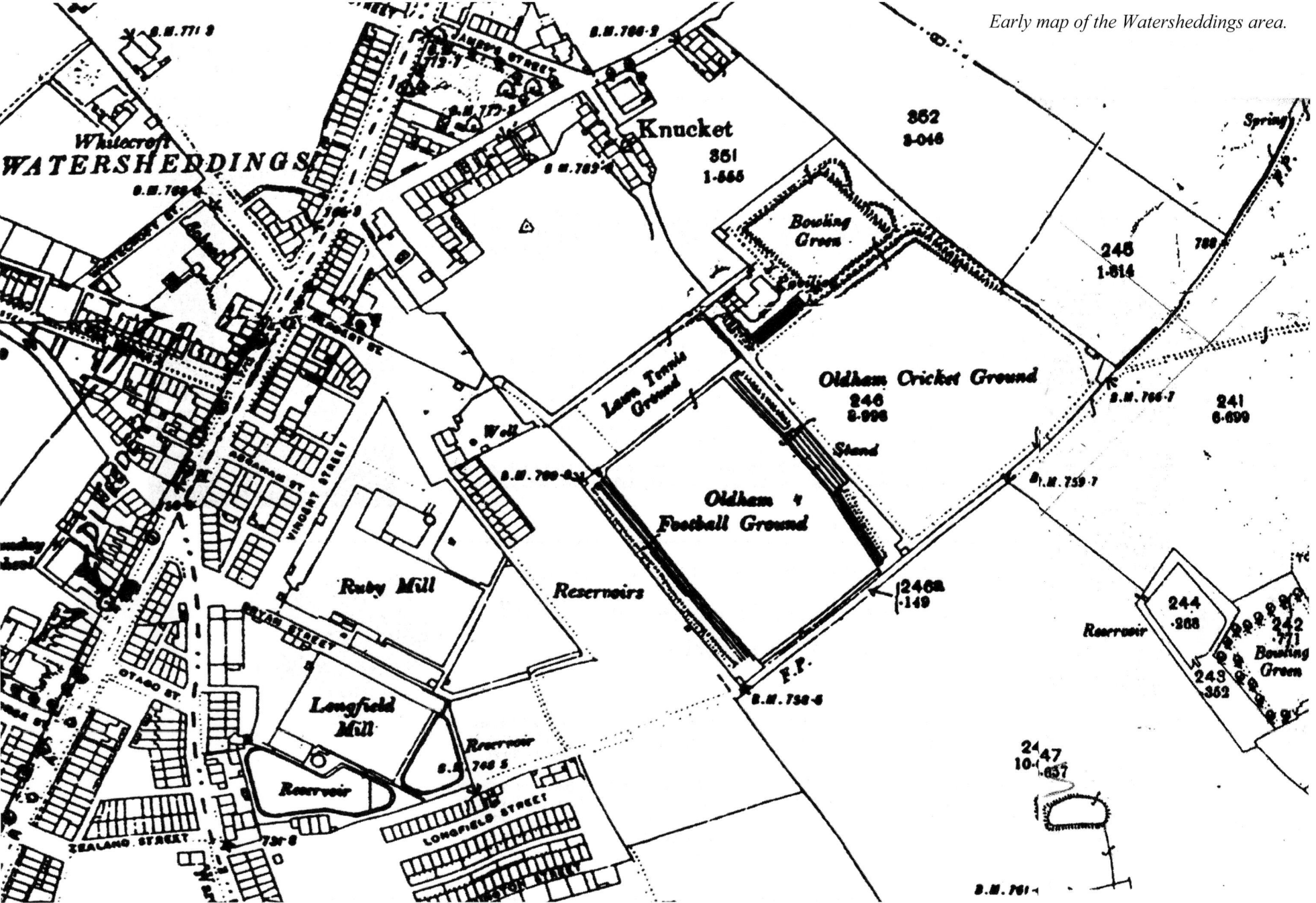

Early map of the Watersheddings area.

The first use of the site for sport was by Oldham Cricket Club who remained at Watersheddings until 1932.

THE C.L.L. CLUBS: OLDHAM

STAMFORD-OLDHAM C.C. WAS ESTABLISHED AT A MEETING AT THE BLACK SWAN HOTEL, MUMPS, IN 1852, LORD STAMFORD BEING THE LANDLORD OF THE FIRST GROUND AT HOLLINHALL.

BETTER THAN STARTIN' WI' A DUCK LAD

BLACK SWAN.

CRICKET. WHAT'S WRONG WI' MARBLES?

FOUNDATION MEMBERS OF C.L.L. IN 1892, RESIGNED 1893, REJOINED 1900, CHAMPIONS 1909 AND 1916

OLDHAM ONCE DISMISSED RAWTENSTALL FOR NINE RUNS.

THEY ALSO PLAYED AT CLARKSFIELD AND WATERSHEDDINGS BEFORE MR. FRANK POLLARD LAID THE KEY SOD OF 'THE POLLARDS' ON MAY 24, 1934.

BOBBY PEEL AND ARTHUR SMITH (22 SEASONS) WERE EARLY 'PROS'.. FOLLOWED BY TED LEYLAND H. WHITEHEAD, R. WHITEHEAD, A.E. LASHBROOK FRED HARTLEY AND AARON LOCKETT.

MASON.

14

FIRST MATCHES AT WATERSHEDDINGS 1889

OLDHAM CRICKET CLUB—JUNE 14th

OLDHAM v. NELSON.—Played at Oldham on Whit-Friday. Score and analysis :—

Nelson.		Oldham.	
W H Bower c Tyack b Smith	25	T Walker c Driver b Willoughby	15
A Hargreaves b Cropper	14	A Smith c Hamon b do	0
R Boys c Holroyd b Smith	1	B Wright b Nutter	4
J Wright run out	18	A Paul c Nutter b Wright	17
W Heap c and b Smith	22	M Cropper st Heap b Stephenson	22
J Driver b Holroyd	3	J Schofield b Wright	0
J Hamon b do	0	C Smethurst run out	0
H Matthews c Wright b do	0	S Taylor b Wright	2
C Nutter c Smith b do	0	A Tyack st Heap b Stephenson	1
F G Willoughby b Smith	8	J K Holroyd not out	1
F Stephenson not out	4	J Mills b Wright	4
Extras	10	Extras	8
Total	105	Total	74

BOWLING ANALYSIS.

Nelson.

	Overs.	Maidens.	Runs.	Wickets.
J K Holroyd	7	5	9	4
Paul	5	1	21	0
Cropper	15	9	24	1
Smith	16·3	4	41	4

Oldham.

Willoughby	11	2	30	2
Nutter	10	4	17	1
Wright	7·3	5	4	4
Stephenson	7	2	15	2

OLDHAM RUGBY CLUB—SEPTEMBER 28th

OLDHAM F.C.

The opening of the Oldham Football Ground on Saturday was an event which was taken advantage of by a large number of people who assembled to witness the encounter between the Swinton team and Oldham.

The number of spectators on the ground when the kick off took place would probably be about 7,000 and the game was watched with keen interest. The ground is well set out and there will be every chance of witnessing brilliant play, when the weather permits. Contrary to expectation the weather was pretty good, very little rain falling during the afternoon, the field of play being in capital condition, notwithstanding the enormous amount of rain that had fallen during the week.

When the teams stepped on to the field a hearty cheer was set up. The Oldham men appearing in their new jerseys, namely red and white. After the preliminaries had been arranged by the team captains it was found that the home team had lost the toss and "Mac" had the honour of setting the ball in motion on the new ground for the first time. Murray replied and the Oldham skipper returned the ball, the first pack being formed in the visitors' territory.

This extract is taken from the Oldham Chronicle match report, which appeared on Monday evening 30th September 1889.

1889

SEASON 1889-90.

"A" TEAM.

DATE.	CLUB.	GROUND
1889.		
Sept. 21	Hollinwood 1st	Away
,, 28	Swinton	Away
Oct. 6	Warrington	Home
,, 12	Dobcross 1st	Away
,, 19		
,, 26	Leeds P. Church	Away
Nov. 2	Widnes............	Away
,, 9	Rochdale Hornets....	Away
,, 16	Rochdale Rangers 1st	Home
,, 23	Manchester Rangers .	Home
,, 30	Tyldesley	Away
Dec. 7	Huddersfield	Home
,, 14	Swinton	Home
,, 21	Chadderton Hrnts. 1st	Away
,, 25	Xmas Day.	
,, 28		
1890.		
Jan. 1		
,, 4	Mossley............	Away
,, 11	Brighouse Rangers ..	Away
,, 18	Tyldesley	Home
,, 25		
Feb. 1	Brighouse Rangers ..	Home
,, 8	Leeds P. Church	Home
,, 15	Chadderton Hrnts. 1st	Home
,, 22	Warrington	Away
Mar. 1	Manchester Rangers .	Away
,, 8	Huddersfield	Away
,, 15	Rochdale Hornets ..	Home
,, 22	Widnes	Home
,, 29	Mossley	Home
,, 31		
Apr. 4	Rochdale Rangers 1st	Away
,, 5	Dobcross 1st	Home
,, 7	Hollinwood 1st	Home

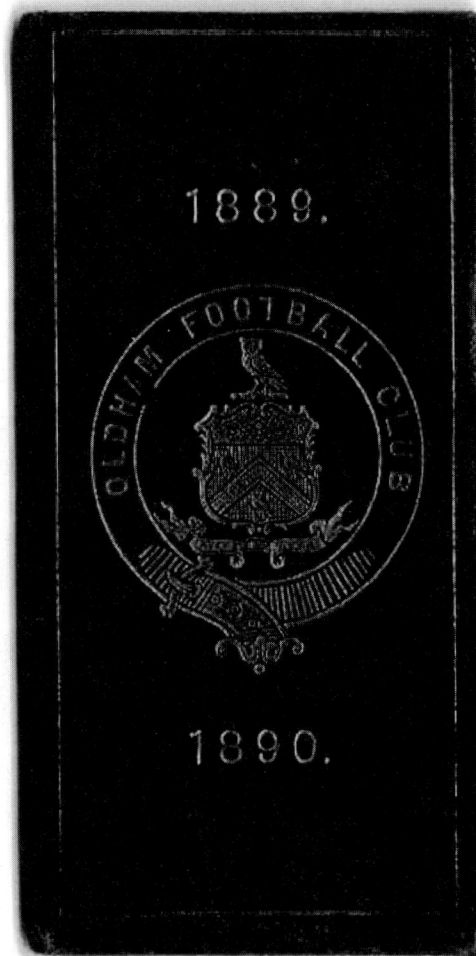

Oldham F.C. member's card for the first season at Watersheddings.

Also see the fixture list for both the first team and reserves ("A" team), whose matches included local opposition against the likes of Chadderton Hornets, Dobcross and Hollinwood.

FIRST TEAM.

DATE.	CLUB.	GROUND
1889.		
Sept. 21	Cleckheaton	Away
,, 28	Swinton	Home
Oct. 5	Warrington	Away
,, 12	Morecambe	Home
,, 19	Leicester	Home
,, 26	Leeds P. Church	Home
Nov. 2	Widnes	Home
,, 9	Rochdale Hornets ..	Home
,, 16	Leicester	Away
,, 23	Manchester Rangers..	Away
,, 30	Tyldesley	Home
Dec. 7	Huddersfield	Away
,, 14	Swinton	Away
,, 21	Cleckheaton	Home
,, 25	Xmas Day—Aspatria .	Home
,, 28		
1890.		
Jan. 1	Heckmondwike	Home
,, 4	Mossley............	Home
,, 11	Brighouse Rangers ..	Home
,, 18	Tyldesley	Away
,, 25	Carlisle	Home
Feb. 1	Brighouse Rangers ..	Away
,, 8	Leeds P. Church	Away
,, 15	St. Helens Recs.	Away
,, 22	Warrington	Home
Mar. 1	Manchester Rangers.	Home
,, 8	Huddersfield	Home
,, 15	Rochdale Hornets ..	Away
,, 22	Widnes	Away
,, 29	Mossley	Away
,, 31	St. Helens Recs.	Home
Apr. 4	Good Fri.—Kendal ..	Home
,, 5	Morecambe	Away
,, 7	Easter Mon.—Carlisle	Away

The Watersheddings pavilion overlooking the cricket pitch, with a centred walkway through the seating area for the team to take the field.

Also, note the balcony which was demolished in the 1950s.

An Oldham team group photographed during the first season at Watersheddings:
Back Row: Darlington, Pendlebury, Giles, Mr. J. Platt (treas.), Holden, Fitton, Simpson.
Middle Row: Mr. S. Taylor (sec.), Armstrong, Bennett, McCutcheon (capt.), Jack Hurst, Pennington, Mr. H. Court (umpire).
Front Row: Blomley, James Hurst, Thomas, Nolan, Gwynne, Nuttall.

Jack Darlington (left) and *Bill Pennington.* *Two members of the Oldham team in the first season at Watersheddings.*

Darlington was a forward and Pennington a three-quarter.

Bill McCutcheon, *wearing his 1891 Wales cap and jersey, and **Ab Ashworth**. Both were internationals while playing for Oldham in the pre Northern Union era. McCutcheon was a member of the first Welsh team to win the "triple crown" in 1893. Ashworth was the only Oldham player to play for England before 1895 and the switch to rugby league.*

Arthur Lees - *here wearing his Lancashire jersey, joined the club in 1892.*

F. Heyhurst (standing) and W. Whitworth Both were members of the "A" team who won the Advertiser Cup in season 1892-93.

1893

OLDHAM CRICKET CLUB FIRST TEAM - SEASON 1893.
23 MATCHES PLAYED, 14 WON, 2 DRAWN, 7 LOST.
Back Row: T. Booth (umpire), D. Horton, A.J. Haworth (hon. sec.), J. S. Hilton, Gascoigne (groundsman), G.P. Sinkinson, J.W. Dunkerley (scorer).
Middle Row: J. Mills, A. Holmes, S. Taylor (capt.), G.N. Smailes, J. Wood, J. Schofield.
Front Row: W. Chadwick, W. Langham, A. Smith.

Oldham "A" Team - Winners of The Advertiser Cup in season 1892-93.
Back Row: *Mr. T. Broome (umpire), T. Holden, R. Cudworth, J. Ballard, J. Platt, J. Hetherington, A. Maylor, W. Whitworth.*
Middle Row: *F. Heyhurst, J. Thomas, S. Lees (capt.), J. Lawton, F. Beaver.*
Front Row: *W. Barnes, J. Wilde, G. Hamer, J. Schofield.*

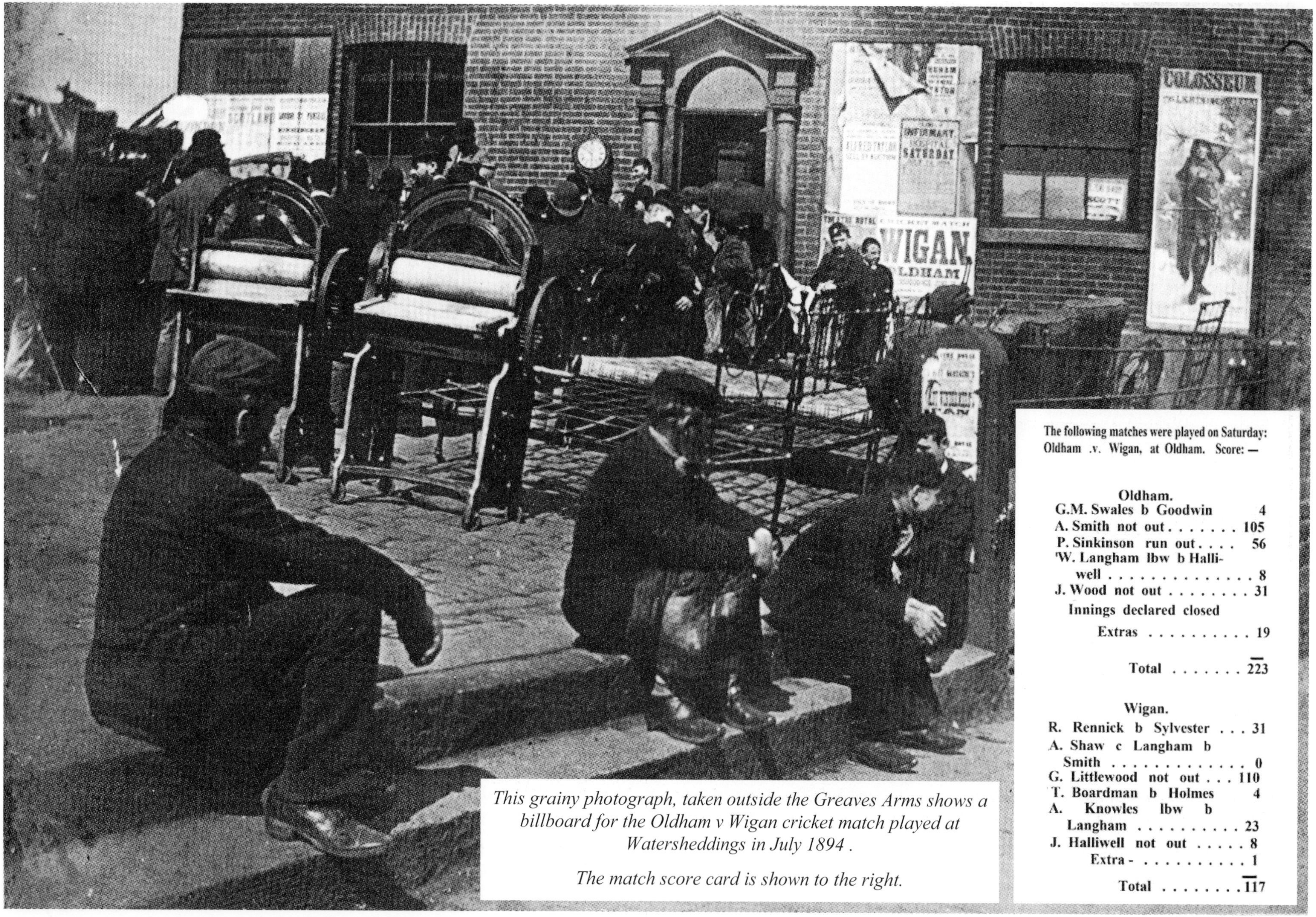

This grainy photograph, taken outside the Greaves Arms shows a billboard for the Oldham v Wigan cricket match played at Watersheddings in July 1894 .

The match score card is shown to the right.

The following matches were played on Saturday:
Oldham .v. Wigan, at Oldham. Score: —

Oldham.

G.M. Swales b Goodwin	4
A. Smith not out	105
P. Sinkinson run out	56
'W. Langham lbw b Halli-well	8
J. Wood not out	31
Innings declared closed	
Extras	19
Total	223

Wigan.

R. Rennick b Sylvester . . .	31
A. Shaw c Langham b Smith	0
G. Littlewood not out . . .	110
T. Boardman b Holmes	4
A. Knowles lbw b Langham	23
J. Halliwell not out	8
Extra -	1
Total	117

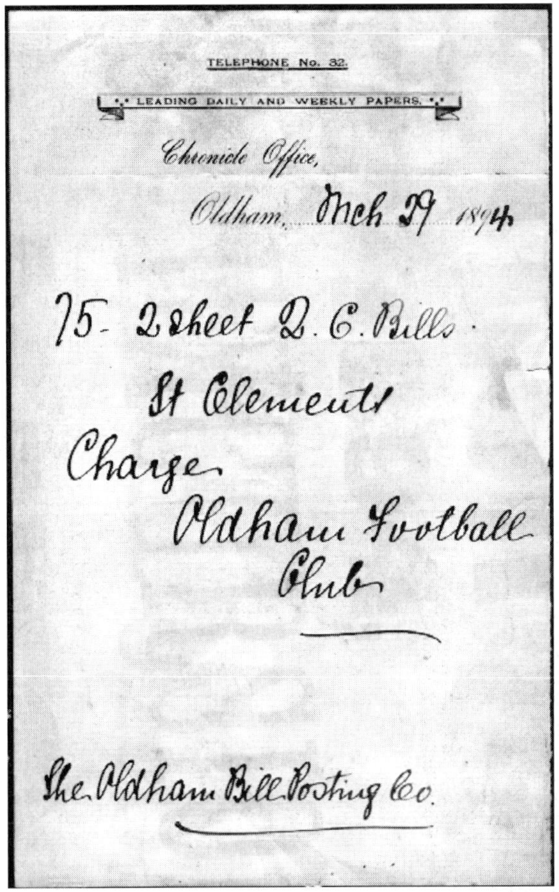

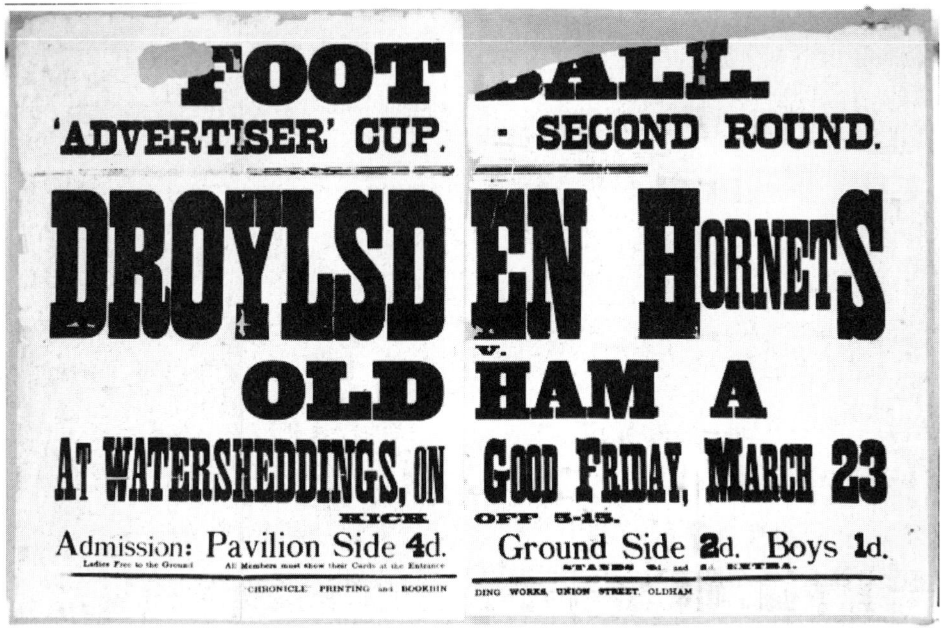

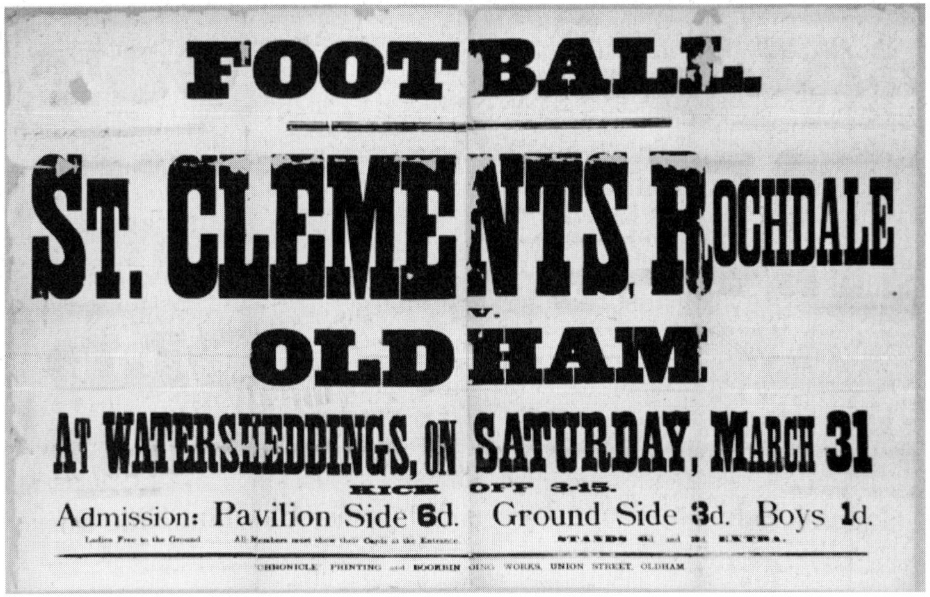

The two posters pictured here have survived from the pre Northern Union days, along with the bill of sale from the Oldham Chronicle who printed them.

The first gives notice of the Oldham "A" team playing against Droylsden Hornets on Good Friday March 23rd 1894 in the Advertiser Cup, of which they were the current holders.

The second advertises the first team match against Rochdale St. Clements eight days later. The dimensions of the these notices were approximately five feet by four feet.

1895

✛ FIRST TEAM. ✛

DATE.	NAME OF CLUB.	GROUND.
Sept. 21	Swansea	Home
23	Huddersfield	Away
28	Halifax	Away
Oct. 5	Leigh	Home
12	St. Helens	Away
19	Tyldesley	Home
26	Wigan	Away
Nov. 2	Batley	Home
9	Huddersfield	Home
16	Edinburgh Wanderers	Home
23	Rockcliffe	Home
30	Widnes	Away
Dec. 7	Stockport	Away
14	Manningham	Home
21	Rochdale Hornets	Home
25		
26	Swansea	Away
28	Runcorn	Home
Jan. 1	Watsonians	Home
4	Bradford	Home
11	Halifax	Home
18	Warrington	Away
25	Broughton Rangers	Home
Feb. 1	Leigh	Away
8	Hartlepool Rovers	Away
15	Tyldesley	Away
18	Bradford	Away
22	Wigan	Home
29	Widnes	Home
March 7	Stockport	Home
14	Rochdale Hornets	Away
21	Warrington	Home
28	Broughton Rangers	Away
April 3		
4	St. Helens	Home
6	Hartlepool Rovers	Home
11	Manningham	Away
18	Runcorn	Away

REVISED FIXTURES.
✛ FIRST TEAM. ✛

DATE.	NAME OF CLUB.	GROUND.
Sept. 14	Hunslet	Away
21	Tyldesley	Home
23	Huddersfield	Away
28	Halifax	Away
Oct. 5	Batley	Home
7	Wakefield Trinity	Home
12	Hull	Away
19	Bradford	Home
26	Widnes	Away
Nov. 2	Manningham	Home
9	Leigh	Away
16	Stockport	Home
23	Warrington	Away
30	Rochdale Hornets	Home
Dec. 7	LANCASHIRE v. YORKSHIRE	Oldham
	Liversedge	Away
14	St. Helens	Home
21	Wigan	Home
25	Broughton Rangers	Home
26	Leeds	Away
28	Warrington	Home
Jan. 1	Brighouse Rangers	Away
4	Runcorn	Away
11	Huddersfield	Home
18	Hunslet	Home
25	Tyldesley	Away
Feb. 1	Halifax	Home
8	Batley	Away
15	Widnes	Home
18	Bradford (Shrove Tuesday)	Away
22	Hull	Home
29	Leigh	Home
March 7	Manningham	Away
14	Stockport	Away
21	Rochdale Hornets	Away
28	Leeds	Home
April 3	Wigan (Good Friday)	Away
4	Brighouse Rangers	Home
6	Liversedge	Home
11	Runcorn	Home
18	St. Helens	Away
22	Wakefield Trinity	Away
25	Broughton Rangers	Away

REVISED FIXTURES.
✛ "A" TEAM. ✛

DATE.	NAME OF CLUB.	GROUND.
Sept. 14		
21	Tyldesley	Away
23		
28	Lees 1st	Home
Oct. 5		
7		
12	Wigan	Home
19	Oldham Victoria	Away
26	Widnes	Home
Nov. 2		
9	Leigh	Home
16	Stockport	Away
23	Warrington	Home
30	Rochdale Hornets	Away
Dec. 7		
14	St. Helens	Away
21	Wigan	Away
25		
26		
28	Warrington	Away
Jan. 1		
4	Runcorn	Home
11	Lees 1st	Away
18		
25	Tyldesley	Home
Feb. 1		
8	St. Helens	Home
15	Widnes	Away
18		
22		
29	Leigh	Away
March 7	Broughton Rangers	Home
14	Stockport	Home
21	Rochdale Hornets	Home
28		
April 3		
4	Brighouse Rangers	Away
6	Broughton Rangers	Away
11	Runcorn	Away
18		
22		
25		

The formation of the Northern Union (later to become known as the Rugby Football League) occurred after a succession of meetings by the prominent northern clubs culminating with the famous breakaway declaration at the George Hotel in Huddersfield on August 29th 1895.

Also shown (above) are the fixtures for the Oldham club, for the first season of the new code and also (left) the original fixtures list before the breakaway.

LANCASHIRE v. YORKSHIRE.

Not alone in Oldham, but all over the North of England, intense interest was taken in the meeting of the chosen representatives of Lancashire and Yorkshire, under the new banner of the Northern Rugby Union, at Watersheddings on Saturday. It was the second county match which had been decided on the splendid ground of the Oldham club, and so far as the local executive were concerned, the arrangements made were such as could not be improved upon. With fair weather there would have been a record attendance, but three days' snowstorms, maintained right up to noon of the day of the encounter, upset all calculations, and the crowd at the start would not be more than 10,000 in number. That very few of these visited the new aerial stand, which was practically ostracised, may be on account of the price, which was fixed by the N.U. Committee for the occasion. Yorkshire had made several changes in their representation from that which did battle against Cheshire, and Lancashire also had a few players who did not assist in the defeat of the Cestrians, these being Hurst, Yates, Cleminson, and Hill. Parkin, of Liversedge, was unable to leave his work in time, and Boothroyd was drafted in, but Sharpe and Wood missed their trains at Low Moor, and it was feared that Sunderland and Cooper, who had donned the jerseys, and along with the rest of the team faced the camera on the bowling green, would have to fill their places, but the late scholars turned up, and at 2 55 the Lancashire team, led by Varley, stepped into the enclosure, followed shortly by the White Rose men, headed by Rigg. Mr. J. Bruckshaw (Stockport) was the referee, and Messrs. H. Sewell (Leeds) and J. E. Warren (Warrington) held the touch flags.

Lancashire: W Winstanley (Wigan), back; F Barber (Warrington), S Lees (Oldham), H C Chapman (Broughton Rangers), and J Hurst (Oldham), threequarter backs; H Varley and A Lees (Oldham), half backs; W Unsworth (Wigan), E Bonser (Oldham), W Briers (St Helens), W Nevens (Warrington), J Worthington (Tyldesley), J Yates (Wigan), T Cleminson (Broughton Rangers), and A Hill (Rochdale Hornets), forwards.

Yorkshire: G E Lorrimer (Manningham), back; B Sharp (Liversedge), L Brooke (Brighouse) Boothroyd (Huddersfield), and F Firth (Halifax), threequarters; A Rigg (Halifax) and R Wood (Liversedge) half backs; N Sutcliffe (Huddersfield) Donkin (Hull), Walton (Wakefield), J Riley (Halifax), O Walsh (Hunslet), T H Hughes (Brighouse), F Cass (Manningham), and R Greig (Leeds), forwards.

Sam Lees   *Jack Hurst*

Harry Varley   *Arthur Lees*   *Emanuel Bonser*

The first ever Northern Union "Roses" match took place at Watersheddings on December 7th 1895 with victory going to Yorkshire by eight points to nil. Oldham had five players in the Lancashire team.

1895

Ben Andrew, born in Oldham, was a forward who played nine times for the Lancashire county side prior to the breakaway from the English Rugby Union.

He was a miner who emigrated to South Africa earlier that year and played for South Africa against the 1896 British touring side.

Harry Broome
137 Appearances
1896-1903

R.L. "Dicky" Thomas
275 Appearances
1897-1909

Herbert Ellis
234 Appearances
1896-1906

Three stalwarts from the early Northern Union days of Oldham F.C.
Forwards Harry Broome and Herbert Ellis along with full-back Dicky Thomas, all
appeared in the Challenge Cup final victory over Hunslet in 1899.

*Forward, Bob Edwards (left) and winger, Tom Martin (middle).
Two recruits from County Durham who played for the club
during the first season of the Northern Union.*

*Local forward Joe Lees (right), another member of the Oldham
squad in that initial breakaway season.*

At the end of the Victorian era Stockport provided Oldham with regular opposition each Christmas. During the match played on Christmas Day 1896 barriers collapsed resulting in improvements to the terracing being carried out. An increase in capacity was achieved and the following year, in the match against Salford, a new record attendance of 20,000 was set.

During this period Oldham born John Bright Davidson was a star forward for the Stockport club and gained county recognition with Cheshire. He later emigrated to Michigan, USA where he became a successful industrialist. His Cheshire kit (pictured here) has survived down the years and is featured in the Rugby League Heritage Centre at the George Hotel, Huddersfield - the birthplace of rugby league.

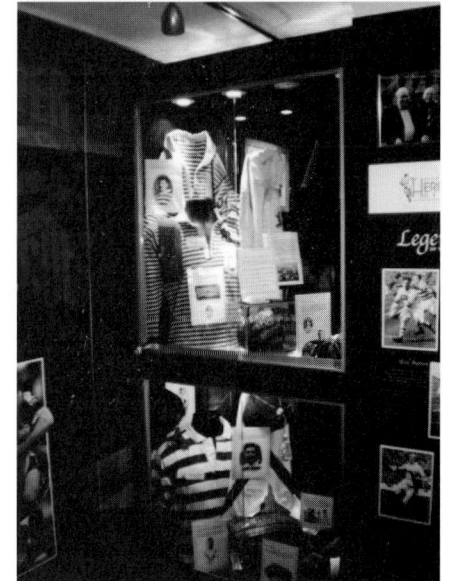

The Oldham "A" team winners of the Advertiser Cup in 1897.

Standing: J. Platt (treas.), F. Wormald, H.B. Byrom, J. Ashton (pres.), I. Chadwick, J. Charnock, J.C. Buckley (sec.), J. Wilkinson, T. Broome (touchjudge).
Seated: A. Kershaw, C. Rennie, G. Walsh, J.W. Whittle, J. Merrill, W. Hoyle, B. Mills, S. Williams.
Kneeling: A. Hall, E. Pearce.

The earliest known image of Oldham playing at Watersheddings circa 1897 / 8.

Oldham Football Club.

President: JAMES ASHTON, Esq.

Annual Dinner,

Friday, May 13th, 1898,

At the TOWN HALL, OLDHAM.

* Menu. *

CLEGG, TYP., OLDHAM.

Wine List.

	Claret.	Bottle	Half-Bottle
1. St. Julien		3/6	2/0
2. Margaux		5/6	3/0
Sparkling and Still Hocks.			
3. Rudesheim		6/0	3/6
4. Sparkling Moselle		5/0	3/0
Burgundy.			
5. Beaune		5/0	3/0
Champagne.			
6. Heidseick		11/0	6/0
7. Moet's		8/6	4/6
8. Bollinger		10/0	5/0
9. Mumm's		9/0	4/6
Port.			
10. Fine Old		5/6	
Sherry.			
11. Fine Sherry		5/6	...

Port and Sherry, per glass		4d.
Spirits, ,,		4d.
Bottled Beer		4d.
Mineral Waters		3d.

Above and opposite - The menu and entertainment programme from the rugby club's annual dinner in 1898, an interesting insight into a social gathering in the late Victorian era.

Menu

Soups.
OX TAIL.   SPRING.

Fish.
HALIBUT. LOBSTER SAUCE.   COD. OYSTER SAUCE.

Entrees.
KIDNEYS AND MUSHROOMS.

STEWED PIGEON.

Joints.
ROAST BEEF.   ROAST LAMB.

ROAST CHICKENS.   BOILED CHICKENS.

HAM AND TONGUE.

Ducklings.

Game.
BLACK GAME.   PTARMIGAN.

Sweets.
PASTRY.   CABINET PUDDING.   CUSTARDS.

WINE JELLIES.   BLANC MANGE.

Cheese and Celery.

Dessert.

Programme.

TOAST..."Queen, Prince and Princess of Wales, and Rest of Royal Family."
Proposed by Mr. JAMES ASHTON.

SONG........."Queen of the Earth"...Mr. W. F. BURTON.

TOAST.. ...."Army, Navy, and Reserve Forces."
Proposed by Mr. R. M. SIXSMITH.

SONG.. .... Mr. M. ASHTON.
Respond : - Captain PATTERSON.

HUMOROUS SKETCH.................Mr. W. CUNLIFFE.

TOAST....................... "Oldham Football Club and Teams "
Proposed by Mr. J. H. HOUGHTON.

SONG.. ...."Ho ! Jolly Jenkin"...Mr. W. F. BURTON.
Respond : - - Mr. J. B. RYE.

HUMOROUS SKETCH .... Mr. W. CUNLIFFE.

TOAST........................ ..."Lancashire Senior Competition."
Proposed by Mr. JAMES ASHTON.

SONG.............. ...., ... Mr. M. ASHTON.
Respond : Mr. J. H. HOUGHTON.

HUMOROUS SKETCH.................... Mr. W. CUNLIFFE.

TOAST............ ...." Town and Trade of Oldham."
Proposed by Mr. E. WARREN.

SONG..."'Neath the Rolling Tide"...Mr. W. F. BURTON.
Respond : His WORSHIPFUL THE MAYOR.

HUMOROUS SKETCH.................Mr. W. CUNLIFFE.

TOAST........ ...." Oldham Cricket Club."
Proposed by Mr. P. S. STOTT.

SONG ... .
Respond : Mr. GEORGE SWAILES.

SONG ....

A famous image of the team outside the pavilion with the Challenge Cup in 1899 when they became the first Lancashire team to lift the renowned trophy.

Back Row: *Bob Edwards, Jim Moffatt, Emanuel Bonser, Herbert Ellis, Arthur Lees (capt.), Harry Broome, Joe Lees, George Frater.*
Middle Row: *Tom Fletcher, Tom Sellars, Dicky Thomas, Sam Lees, Tom Davies.*
Front Row: *Tom Martin, Sam Williams, Joe Lawton, William Barnes.*

A trio of Scottish forwards who played for Oldham at the turn of the Victorian era.

Above left: George Frater
Above right: Jim Moffatt
Right: E.W. (Jim) Telfer.

Sam Williams who scored an amazing 47 tries during the 1900-01 season.
This was a staggering total in the early days of the Northern Union.

JULY 23rd 1900

SMITH TAKES ALL TEN WICKETS FOR OLDHAM

In taking all ten Royton wickets playing for Oldham, Arthur Smith recorded the magnificent bowling figures of 10 for 47.

CENTRAL LANCASHIRE LEAGUE.
ROYTON v OLDHAM.

At Royton.

ROYTON.

Ingleby b Smith	74
W Charnock c and b Smith	6
F Dixon b Smith	11
Z Chester b Smith	2
Littlewood b Smith	6
J Tattersall b Smith	2
F O Holden c Arundale b Smith	5
E Dyer not out	9
J H Holden b Smith	0
E Stott b Smith	0
T Eastwood b Smith	5
Extra	1
Total	**121**

OLDHAM

G Potter l Dixon	58
Smith c Charnock b Littlewood	6
Dr Wood b Dixon	37
A Mills not out	7
A Marall c Eastwood b Littlewood	1
G Rhodes not out	42
Extras	13
Total for four wickets)	**164**

Arthur Smith, was the Oldham C.C. professional for 22 consecutive seasons from 1884 to 1905.

During his Oldham career, he amassed 13,058 runs and took 1,560 wickets. One of the most notable cricketers of his day, he also played in 47 first class matches for Lancashire, scoring some 1,416 runs and taking 29 wickets.

The first rugby match at Watersheddings in 1889, featured Oldham and Swinton.

The images here and over the page are taken from a match against the same opponents on 12th January 1901. This was also the first moving image captured on film of an Oldham team in action.

Joe Lawton is seen feeding the scrum, with Arthur Lees at the base and Tom Fletcher waiting to receive the ball.
Result: Oldham 5 Swinton 7.

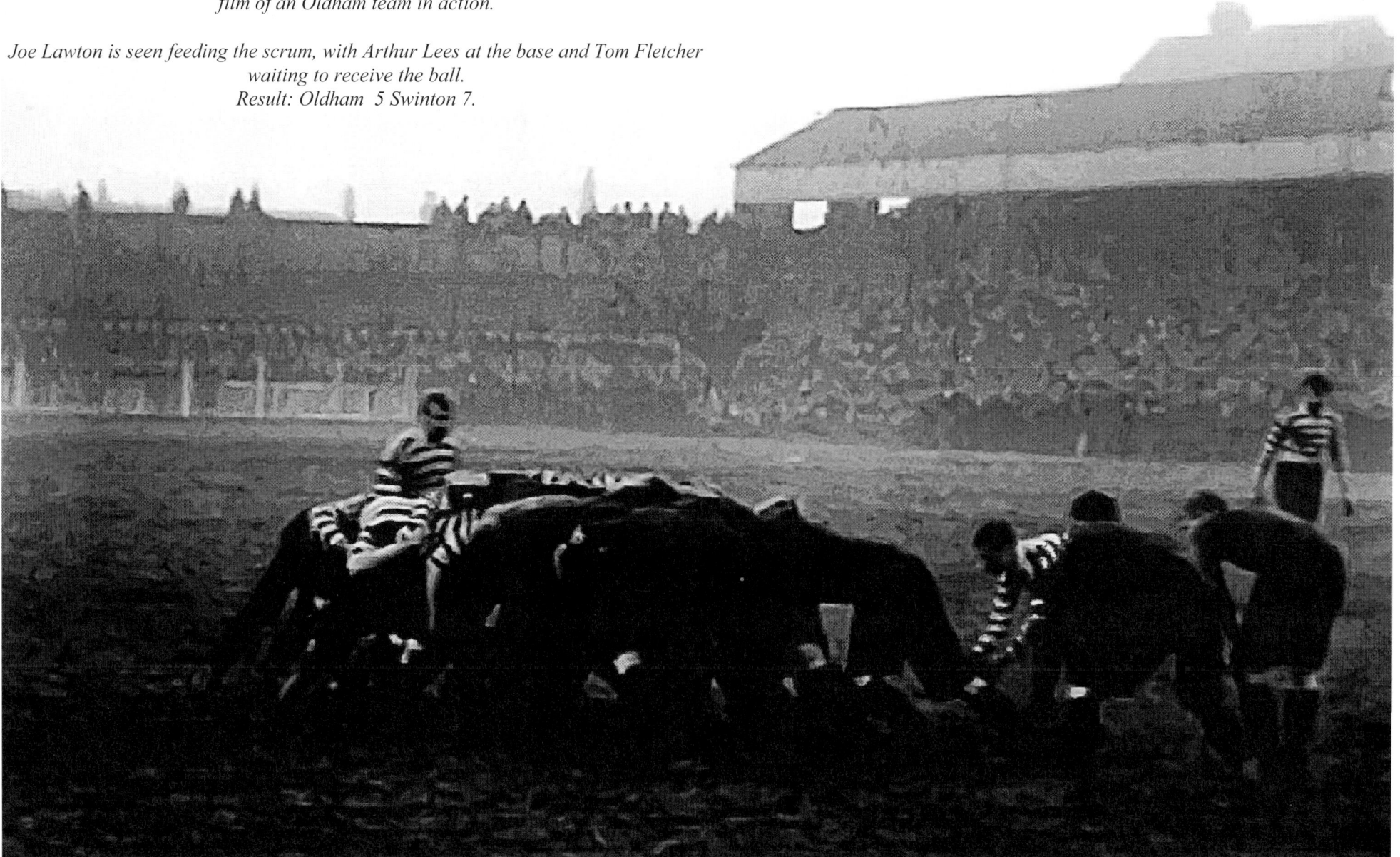

1901

*Right: Tom Davies who scored the only
Oldham try in this match.
The Roughyeds lost the original
encounter by seven points to five.*

*However, the replay ended in a draw
three points each with Davies again
scoring the Oldham try.*

*A result which come the season's end
gave Oldham the Lancashire league title
by a one point advantage over the Lions.*

*Above: Further action from the same match, which was abandoned
due to the massive crowd (21,294) spilling over on to the pitch.
The game was replayed on 25th February 1901.*

*Right: A section of the crowd at the match against Swinton.
Note the number of ladies, dressed in their best, for what must have
been quite a "must see" social occasion as well as being an
important rugby fixture.*

A third image from the abandoned game against Swinton in January 1901.

1901

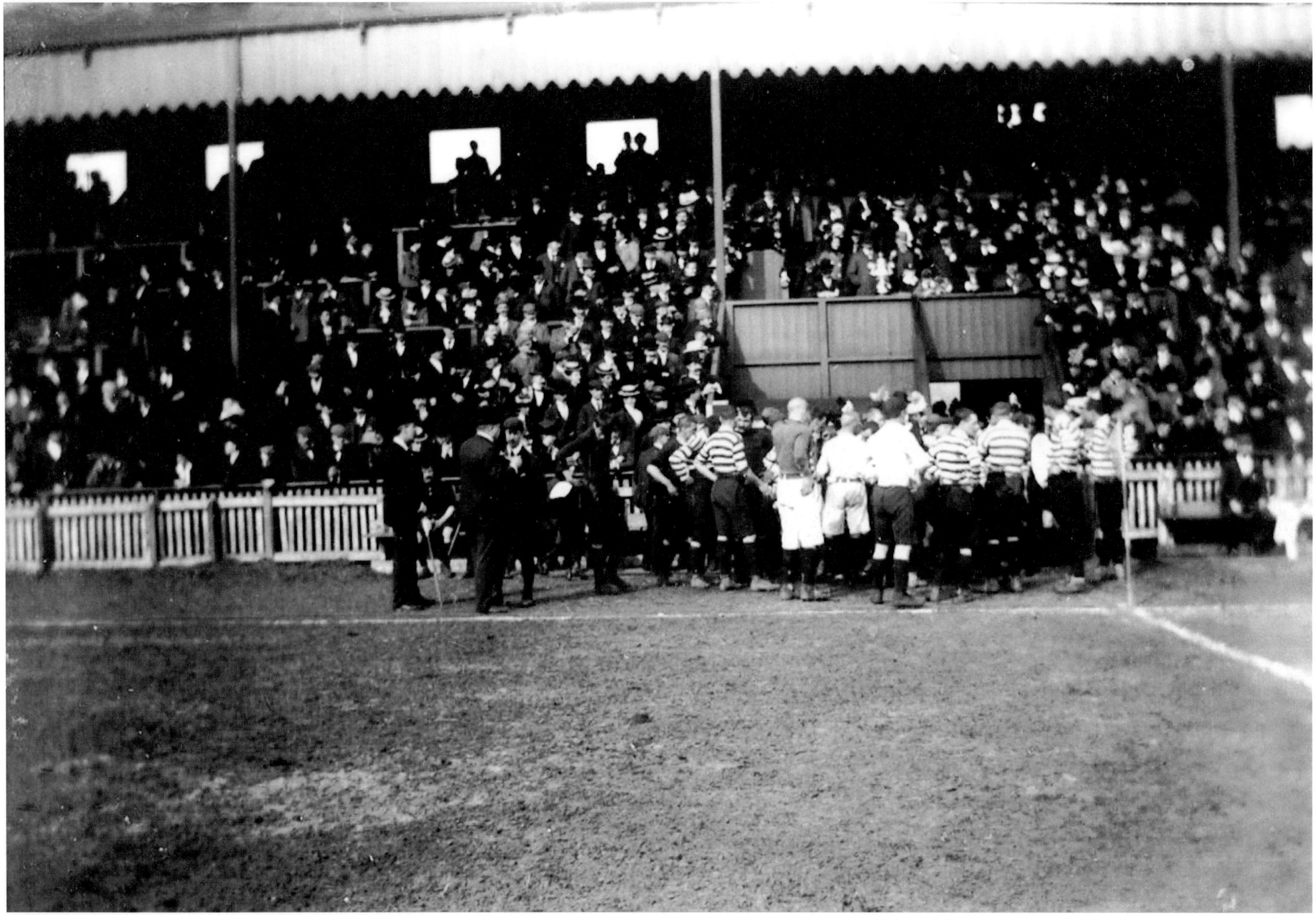

On April 20th 1901 Oldham F.C., the newly crowned Lancashire League champions, took on the "Rest of the League" at Watersheddings before a crowd of 10,000 spectators.

The match went to the Roughyeds by nine points to five with the Oldham points coming from three tries. One for winger, Charlie Civil and two from captain, Arthur Lees.

After the game the Lancashire League Trophy was presented to the Oldham captain, with the moment being captured in the images here and opposite.

1902 saw the debut of local born wingers,
George Tyson *(left) and* **Tommy Cash.**

Tyson scored over 100 tries in 246 games for the Roughyeds and was the hero of the first test series against the Australians in 1908, scoring a try in each test.

Cash played in 139 first team matches for Oldham scoring 63 tries.

More action from Watersheddings in the early 1900s.

FOOTBALL

A NEW COMPETITION

"OLDHAM STANDARD" CHALLENGE CUP

The proprietors of the "Oldham Standard" have shown a practical interest in the development of local junior football. In other words they have offered to provide a £50 challenge cup for competition by the Rugby junior teams within a radius of seven or eight miles of Oldham. The members of the winning team will each receive a gold medal valued at £1 and the runners-up will be awarded medals to the value of 12s 6d each. The competition shall be played with teams of twelve a-side and it was hoped that the cup would be a great success and the means of giving pleasure to spectators and players alike for many years to come.

George Hutchins appointed as the first secretary for the "Oldham Standard Challenge Cup" committee.

"OLDHAM STANDARD" CHALLENGE CUP

FIRST ROUND DRAW

Heyside v Central Rangers
Oldham Edge v Melrose
Lees v Salem Rangers
Glodwick Juniors v Pendleton Britannia
Neville Hornets v Salford St Barts
Rochdale Athletic v Abbey Hills
Byes—Rochdale Rangers and Egerton

FINAL

HEYSIDE……………...9

ROCHDALE
RANGERS……………...0

ATTENDANCE   4,000 EST

"STANDARD" CHALLENGE CUP.

THE FINAL TIE.

HEYSIDE'S EASY VICTORY.

PRESENTATION OF TROPHY AND MEDALS.

The "Oldham Standard" Challenge Cup has been won and lost. The final tussle was a most interesting one, both to the players and the spectators. And there was a gratifying number of the latter on the Oldham ground at Water-sheddings—4,000 at least. No doubt there would have been many more onlookers, but for the fact that the idea had spread abroad that owing to

and the forwards made a plucky attempt but the Heyside defending trio proved too strong. A retaliatory rush was led by the Heyside left wing forwards, who feeding their three-quarters just at the proper moment, were instrumental in inaugurating a sortie which all but proved successful. Rawson, however, came to the rescue at the psychological moment. Play had again become exciting where the ball went into touch and Heyside were awarded a free kick

STANDARD CUP FINAL RESULTS

1904	Heyside	9	:	0	Rochdale Rangers
1905	Rochdale Rangers	7	:	0	Salford St. Bartholemhew's
1906	Radcliffe Rangers	2	:	0	Rochdale Rangers
1907	Heyside	13	:	10	Rochdale Rangers
1908	Leigh Rangers	4	:	3	Egerton
1909	St. Mary's CYMS	12	:	0	Luzley Brook
1910	Broadway St. Ind.	19	:	2	Rochdale St. George
1911	Rochdale St.George	7	:	0	St. Mary's CYMS
1912	Ashton-Under-Lyne	3	;	0	Heyside United Sunday Schools
1913	Healey Street Adults	33	;	0	Prestwich Church
l914	lHealey Street Adults	8	:	0	Pendleton
1915	Wardley	12	:	0	Swinton Park

1916 to 1919 - Competition Suspended

| 1920 | Swinton Park | 17 | : | 5 | Pendleton |
| 1921 | Swinton Park | 10 | : | 2 | Healey Street Adults |

(After extra time - 2:2 after normal time)

1922	Wardley	10	:	3	Pendlebury Juniors
1923	Pendlebury Juniors	4	:	2	Smallbridge Recreation
1924	Smallbridge Recreation	17	:	3	Sandfield Hornets
1925	Healey Street Adults	11	:	0	Crossfield

1926 Sandfield Hornets were awarded the Cup-Chloride Recreation and
Crossfield did not play their semi-final within the stipulated period

1927	Swinton St. Peter's	16	:	3	Seedley Rangers
1928	Swinton Juniors	13	:	2	Highermoor
1929	Higginshaw	3	:	3	Chloride Recreation

Higginshaw were awarded the cup(Chloride Recreation left the
field after eight minutes of the replay, the score at 0 : 0)

1930	Higginshaw	7	:	7	Salem Hornets
	Higginshaw	9	:	0	Salem Hornets
1931	Higginshaw	16	:	3	Salem Hornets
1932	Higginshaw	16	:	0	Saddleworth Rangers
1933	Higginshaw	26	:	3	Strinesdale
1934	Saddleworth Rangers	5	:	4	Higginshaw
1935	Greenacres	5	:	5	Higginshaw

Greenacres were awarded the cup (Higginshaw failed to appear for the
replay after a dispute with the league concerning the match receipts)

1936	Greenacres	9	:	5	Higginshaw
1937	Ferranti	28	;	2	Greenacres
1938	Ferranti	11	:	9	Saddleworth Rangers
1939	Higginshaw	9	:	5	Ferranti

1940 to 1945 competition suspended

1946	Platts Hartford Works	16	:	7	Waterhead
1947	Higginshaw	16	:	4	Ferranti
1948	Higginshaw	21	:	7	Greenacres
1949	Higginshaw	12	:	4	Waterhead
1950	Greenacres	6	:	4	Higginshaw
1951	Greenacres	14	:	0	Lowermoor

1952	Higginshaw	10	:	9	Saddleworth Rangers
1953	Higginshaw	5	:	0	Saddleworth Rangers
1954	Lowermoor	23	:	15	Milnrow
1955	Saddleworth Rangers	8	:	7	Saint Mary's
1956	Sadddleworth Rangers	11	:	10	Saint Anne's
1957	Royton	17	:	4	Saint Mary's
1958	Royton	15	:	3	Higginshaw
1959	Royton	9	:	5	Higginshaw
1960	Higginshaw	16	:	11	Saddleworth Rangers
1961	Langworthy Juniors	12	:	8	Mayfield
1962	Saint Anne's	17	:	9	Saddleworth Rangers
1963	Saddleworth Rangers	20	:	0	Saint Mary's
1964	Saint Mary's	2	:	0	Langworthy Juniors
1965	Saint Anne's	10	:	6	Saint Mary's
1966	Saint Mary's	8	:	2	Langworthy Juniors
1967	Saddleworth Rangers	9	:	0	Saint Mary's
1968	Saint Anne's	23	:	2	Langworthy Juniors
1969	Langworthy Juniors	19	:	3	Saint Anne's
1970	Saint Anne's	6	:	6	Langworthy Juniors
	Saint Anne's	16	:	10	Langworthy Juniors
1971	Saddleworth Rangers	20	:	8	Saint Anne's
1972	Mayfield	18	:	3	Waterhead
1973	Mayfield	24	:	2	Waterhead
1974	Saint Anne's	22	:	0	Ferranti
1975	Mayfield	11	:	5	Higginshaw
1976	Saddleworth Rangers	16	:	4	Waterhead
1977	Saint Anne's	30	:	0	Higginshaw
1978	Saint Anne's	18	:	7	Saddleworth Rangers
1979	Mayfield	11	:	11	Saint Anne's
	Mayfield	8	:	0	Saint Anne's
1980	Saddleworth Rangers	11	:	8	Saint Anne's
1981	Waterhead	9	:	7	Saddleworth Rangers
1982	Waterhead	9	:	6	Saint Anne's
1983	Saddleworth Rangers	9	:	5	Fitton Hill
1984	Mayfield	25	:	2	Shaw
1985	Fitton Hill	9	:	8	Shaw
1986	Waterhead	13	:	8	Mayfield
1987	Saint Anne's	38	:	18	Saddleworth Rangers
1988	Saint Anne's	16	:	14	Saddleworth Rangers
1989	Saint Anne's	22	:	6	Saddleworth Rangers
1990	Saddleworth Rangers	13	:	8	Saint Anne's
1991	Saddleworth Rangers	26	:	14	Saint Anne's
l992	Saddleworth Rangers	22	:	8	Waterhead
l993	Saint Anne's	16	:	12	Waterhead
l994	Higginshaw	10	:	2	Waterhead
l995	Saint Anne's	18	:	10	Saddleworth
1996	Saddleworth Rangers	22	:	12	Higginshaw

The Oldham Championship winning team of 1904-05
Back Row: Harry Topham, Dai Thomas, Adam Jardine, Herbert Ellis, Arthur Lees, Harry Vowles, George Frater, Jim Wright, Arthur Glossop (trainer).
Middle Row: Tom White, Joe Wilkinson, Tom Sellars, George Tyson, Charlie Civil, Sam Lees, Joe Owens, Rueben Carpenter.
Front Row: Dicky Thomas, Frank Spottiswoode, Tommy Cash, David Lewis, Tom McLean, Joe Lawton.

The 1906-07 season saw the number of players in each team reduced to thirteen and so this new defining shape of the Northern Union gave rise to the rugby league code we know today.

The season did not start well for Oldham with a home defeat to Runcorn. However, it would be another 60 matches and some two and a half years before the Roughyeds colours were lowered at Watersheddings again.

Below an Oldham line up of the time.

Back Row: *George Tyson, Tommy Cash, Billy Dixon.*
Second Row: *Billy Longworth, Arthur Smith, Jim Wright, Joe Wilkinson, Joe Ferguson.*
Third Row: *Bert Avery, Tom White, Arthur Lees, Tom McLean, Joe Owens.*
Front: *Dicky Thomas.*

GEORGE W. SMITH

SPRINTER   HURDLER   APPRENTICE JOCKEY

TRY SCORING WINGER!

1887. APPRENTICED JOCKEY. WON SEVERAL RACES AND PLAYED HALF-BACK FOR STABLE BOYS TEAM IN AND AROUND AUCKLAND

1895. JOINED AUCKLAND CITY F.C. AS FULL BACK OR CENTRE. SPEED MADE HIM A NATURAL WINGER. TOURED AUSTRALIA 1896-97

ON THE TRACK, BECAME KNOWN AS 'THE GREYHOUND'. WAS 100 YARDS SPRINT CHAMPION OF NEW ZEALAND FIVE TIMES, 1898 TO 1904, 120 YARDS HURDLES FOUR TIMES AND 440 HURDLES FIVE TIMES. IN 1899-1900 HELD NEW ZEALAND CHAMPIONSHIP FOR 100 & 120 YARDS FLAT AND 120 & 440 YARDS HURDLES. ONE OF THE ORIGINAL "ALL BLACKS". CAME TO ENGLAND WITH BASKERVILLES N.Z. TEAM OF 1908. SIGNED FOR OLDHAM AT CLOSE OF TOUR, WHEN 34 YEARS OF AGE. SCORED 37 TRIES 1911-12. WON 2 NORTHERN LEAGUE MEDALS AND 2 LANCS COUNTY MEDALS. A BROKEN LEG ENDED HIS BRILLIANT CAREER IN 1916. BECAME CLUB TRAINER, AND LIVED IN OLDHAM UNTIL HIS DEATH, DEC. 7, 1954, AGED 80 YEARS.

New Zealand $1.50
GEORGE SMITH ALBERT BASKERVILLE
EARLY RUGBY LEAGUE

1907 saw the first visit of an international touring team to Watersheddings.
The New Zealand "All Golds", as they came to be known because of their professionalism, played at Watersheddings on November 23rd, when the Roughyeds recorded an eight points to seven victory.

At the conclusion of the tour, George (G.W.) Smith signed for Oldham. An all-round sportsman of some repute, Smith was a champion sprinter, hurdler and jockey as well as having toured with the 1905 "All Blacks" rugby union team.

His achievements have been recognised in his own country by his inclusion in the New Zealand sporting "Hall of Fame" and he appeared on the national stamp in 1995 in celebration of the centenary of the Rugby League.

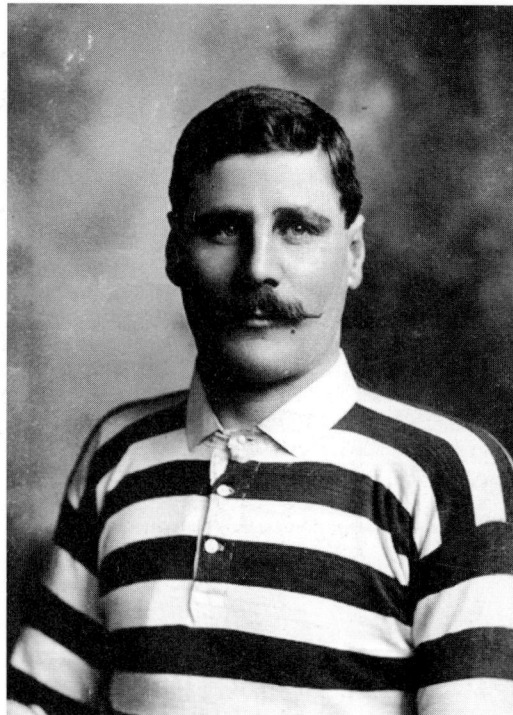

OLDHAM R.F.C. PAST v PRESENT.

On April 20th 1908 a match took place between Oldham "Past v Present" as a benefit match for Emanuel Bonser and E.R. Porter.
On the extreme left and right of the back row are ex players Jack Hurst and Alfred Tetlow with Bill McCutcheon who refereed the match in the centre.

1909

International half-backs, Tom White of England and
Albert Anlezark of Australia, photographed outside
the bowls pavilion in 1909 and also in their
international colours.

CRICKET.

CENTRAL LANCASHIRE LEAGUE.

OLDHAM WIN THE CUP.

The match at Watersheddings on Saturday decided the championship of the Central Lancashire League, and Oldham's victory gave them the right to hold the cup for the first time in their history. It has been a keen struggle all through the season and Glossop were rather more unfortunate in respect of weather than Oldham were, though both clubs suffered loss of probable points from this cause. The opposition last Saturday at Watersheddings was provided by Middleton, who, batting in drizzling rain, made a very feeble resistance to the attack of Lynes and Binns, and were tumbled out for the small total of 40. Lynes took six wickets for 20 runs, a very fine winding up to his season; and Binns took four for 19. Although the Oldham men made a poor start, losing two wickets for 15 runs, they easily managed to overtake the visitors' score with only three wickets down, and when the match was won the game was not proceeded with further. Mr. Josiah Greenhalgh, the president of the club, made a short speech congratulating the team on their season's success, and subsequently entertained the Oldham and Middleton players and a party of friends at the Cafe Monico.

MIDDLETON.

W. Pink b Lynes	3
T. Butterworth c Walker b Binns	1
Cassley c Potter (G.) b Lynes	8
F. W. Hampson c Hilton b Lynes	3
J. Ogden not out	13
F. Mills c Wood b Binns	1
H. R. Ramsbottom c Horton b Lynes	0
H. Kinder b Lynes	1
A. Capper (Junr.) b Binns	1
A. E. Kay lbw b Binns	0
J. H. Wood c Whitehead b Lynes	8
Extra	1
Total	40

OLDHAM.

Robinson not out	26
Lynes b Ogden	3
Binns c Pink b Cassley	10
H. Horton c Ogden b Cassley	2
Dr. Wood not out	7
Total (for three wickets)	48

Oldham C.C. claimed the Central Lancashire League title for the first time in 1909.

CENTRAL LANCASHIRE LEAGUE.
FINAL TABLE
FIRST DIVISION.

	Pld.	Won.	Lost.	Drn.	Pts.
Oldham	24	12	1	11	35
Glossop	24	11	1	12	34
Royton	24	10	3	11	31
Crompton	24	7	2	15	29
Stalybridge	24	6	7	11	23
Moorside	24	5	6	13	23
Dukinfield	24	7	9	8	22
Middleton	24	3	6	15	21
Rochdale	24	6	9	2	21
Milnrow	24	6	9	9	21
Littleborough	24	6	10	8	20
Walsden	24	3	10	11	17
Heywood	24	3	12	9	15

OLDHAM. C.C.

AVERAGES 1909

FIRST ELEVEN

Matches arranged 24— Won 12, viz.: Middleton twice, Milnrow twice, Walsden twice, Littleborough twice, Heywood twice, Rochdale and Moorside.

Lost 1—Rochdale.

Drawn 7, viz.: Glossop twice, Crompton twice, Royton, Dukinfield and Moorside.

Not played owing to rain—4, viz.: Stalybridge twice, Royton and Dukinfield.

Total runs scored by Oldham 2,972 for 128 wickets; average per wicket 23.21.

Total runs scored by opponents 2,153 for 168 wickets; average 12.82.

Scores of 100 and over: J. F. Robinson *142; J. Lynes, 120; G. Potter *102.

Scores of 50 and over: J. F. Robinson, 54, 73, 93, 50; J. Lynes, 59*, 79; B. Walker, 68*, 68; G. Potter, 69; J. T. Binns, 61; C. Mildenhall, 60

BATTING.

	Inns.	Most in an inns.	Total runs.	Avge.
G. Potter	16	*102	410	34.13
J. F. Robinson	20	*142	613	34.05
J. Lynes	18	121	529	33.06
B. Walker	15	*68	359	27.61
C. Mildenhall	14	60	227	22.75
Dr. J. Wood	12	49	165	18.33
S. S. Potter	12	44	160	18.00
H. Horton	7	47	84	14.00
J. T. Binns	15	61	181	12.92
W. Whitehead	7	37	75	10.71
J. R. Lawton	6	*13	30	7.50
L. Dransfield	5	7	19	6.33

BOWLING.

	Overs.	Runs.	Wkts.	Avge.
H. Horton	25	39	6	6.50
G. Potter	149	420	40	10.50
C. Mildenhall	112	274	24	11.41
J. Lynes	245	643	54	11.90
J. T. Binns	190	486	34	14.29

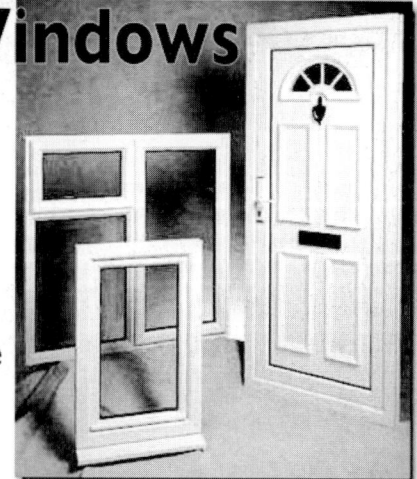

The Oldham team and officials 1909-10 League Champions and Lancashire Cup winners.
Back Row: J.D. Blunn, W. McCutcheon, P. Ingham, A. Lees, W.H. Buckley, A.E. Tetlow, H. Langton, R. Thompson, D.H. Rhodes, C. Hutchins.
Second Row: S. Williams, T. Sellars, J. Wiltshire, W. Dixon, A. Avery, T. McCabe, A. Smith, W. Jardine, W. Young, F. Wise, G. Kilner (sec.).
Third Row: T. McLean, G. Tyson, G. Cook, S. Deane, J. Ferguson, J. Platt (pres.), J. Wright, "B". Dixon, J. Lomas, A. Wood.
Front Row: T. White, J. Wharton, G.W. Smith, J. Owens, E.A. Anlezark.

1910

TOUR REPRESENTATIVES

Oldham had two players selected for the first ever tour to Australia and New Zealand.
Bert Avery and Tom Helm were both forwards and whereas Avery had a most successful trip scoring a hat-trick in the one test against New Zealand, the unfortunate Helm was taken ill en-route and didn't play in any of the matches.

Avery can be seen on the extreme right of the front row in the team group.

Tom Helm

Albert Avery

This photograph was taken on the occasion of the home debut of Jim Lomas playing for Oldham against Runcorn on February 11th, 1911. His first match for the Roughyeds on the previous week had been against his former club Salford.
On this day, Lomas, who captained the first ever tour to Australia in 1910, obliged the Oldham supporters with two tries in a 21 - 10 victory. Here he is seen about to release the ball to his winger Billy Dixon. Also in the photograph are Sid Deane and Joe Ferguson.

1912

When Oldham reached the Challenge Cup final in 1912 against Dewsbury, the local officials were so confident of victory that an illuminated tram was organised to greet the winners on their return. However, no one told the Yorkshiremen who spoiled the show with an eight points to five reverse for the Roughyeds at Headingley.

Here we see a hand-bill produced by the Dewsbury club showing ticket and travel details.

Above left: **George Cook,** who scored the Oldham try in the 1912 Challenge Cup final.
Above right: **Bert Avery,** controversially dismissed in the second half when Oldham were actually ahead in the game.

NORTHERN UNION CUP. FINAL.
Dewsbury Northern Union Football Club.
Headquarters - SCARBRO' HOTEL.

Saturday, April 27th, 1912.
DEWSBURY
VERSUS
OLDHAM
AT HEADINGLEY, LEEDS.

E. J. JACKETT

¾ Backs	W. RHODES
	E. WARE
	E. WARD
	G. SHARPLES
½ Backs	T. MILNER
	J. NEARY
Forwards	F. RICHARDSON
	P. O'NEILL
	G. A. GARNETT
	J. HAMMILL
	A. V. ABBISHAW
	A. EVANS

Kick off 3-30

ADMISSION 1s. BOYS 6d.

Stands 2s.

Reserved Seats, including admission to the Ground. 5/- each.

Application for same, which in all cases must be accompanied by remittance, to be made to

J. GOLDTHORPE,
The Pavilion. Headingley, Leeds.

EXCURSIONS L. & N.W.
12-30, 1-7, 1-30, 1-39, 2-10, 2-25 p.m.

FARE 1s.

Tickets may be had in advance at ALTHAMS, MARKET PLACE, DEWSBURY.

Ambler & Peate, Printers, Northgate, Dewsbury.

Tommy Brice & Joe Ferguson photographed in training.

At this time half-back Brice was captain of the "A" team with Ferguson the skipper of the first team.

1913

Oldham v Dewsbury September 6th, 1913.
Back Row: *Charlie Waye, Dave Holland, Bert Avery, Joe Ferguson, Charlie Robeson, Jim Wright, George W. Smith.*
Front Row: *Evan Davies, Viv Farnsworth, Billy Hall, Albert E. Anlezark, Jim Parkinson, Billy Farnsworth, Tom Williams.*

60

"Joe Ferguson's Dreadnoughts" reads the sign above the bus as the Oldham team arrive at Clegg Street station before boarding a train to an away match.

OLDHAM FOOTBALL CLUB.
COLONIAL TOURISTS and PRESIDENT 1914.

PHOTO, HAIGH.   OLDHAM.

TOUR REPRESENTATIVES

Oldham had three players selected for the 1914 tour to Australia and New Zealand, all of whom were selected for the famous third and deciding match which has become known as the Rorke's Drift test. They are pictured here with club president Mr. R. Thompson.

Billy Hall *(standing)*
Alf Wood *(left)*
Dave Holland *(right)*

Full-back Wood played a particularly significant part in the 14 - 6 victory for the depleted Lions by way of his four goals and heroics as the last line of defence.

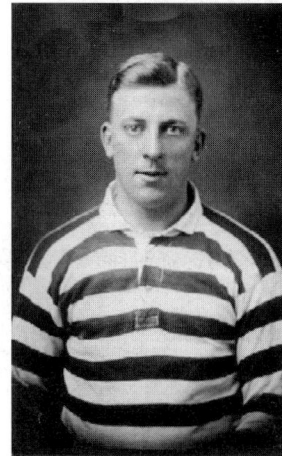  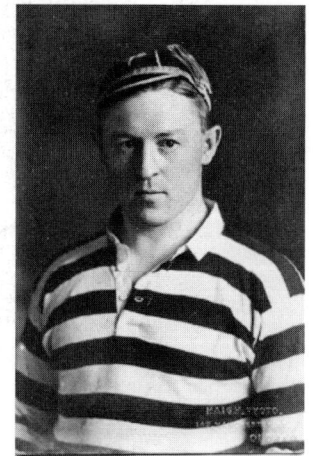

Billy Hall   *Dave Holland*   *Alf Wood*

Four Oldham players in "civvies" during the 1914 -1915 season, left to right: Alf Edwards, Billy Hall, Jack Bedwelty Jones and Billy Jardine.

The First World War.
This photograph shows ironically thirteen Oldham players along with their officers who enlisted in the 2nd / 10th Battalion of the Manchester regiment in April 1915.
Back Row: Pte. C. Waye, Pte. W. Jardine, Pte. J. Tetlow, Sgt. E. Oliver, Pte. "B". Dixon, Sgt. H. Carter.
Middle Row: Sgt. A.D. West, Sgt. T. Brice, Sgt-Maj. F.W. Wise. Colonel W. Patterson, Colonel C. Hodgkinson, QM Sgt. V. Farnsworth. Sgt. J.S. Parkinson
Front Row: Pte. T. White, Pte. T.O. Jones.

OLDHAM F.C.

OFFICIAL PROGRAMME.

Northern Rugby Football Union

CUP FINAL.

HUDDERSFIELD

v.

ST. HELENS

ON SATURDAY, MAY 1st, 1915,

At Watersheddings,

KICK-OFF AT 3-30 PROMPT.

EVENING CHRONICLE, SATURDAY, MAY 1, 1915

Northern Union Cup

Final Tie at Watersheddings

HUDDERSFIELD v. ST. HELENS.

For the first time the Oldham F.C. ground was today the venue of the final tie for the Challenge Cup of the Northern Union, and it was expected that, owing to the depression which has fallen upon the attendances at all the football encounters, the ground would prove amply big enough to accommodate all the spectators who wished to attend. The holding capacity of the ground was not likely to be tested, for, though a good number of followers might be expected to come from Huddersfield, it was not considered likely that there would be any great influx from St. Helens, owing to the greater distance and the fact that there is a good deal of Government work going on in that district.

The teams which had qualified to meet in the final were Huddersfield and St. Helens, and, though the appearance of the latter at this advanced stage of the competition had been quite a

Wagstaff and company were quickly on the warpath again—and

SCORING RAPIDLY.

Rosenfeld on one wing and then Wagstaff on the other scored in brilliant style, and Gronow improved the first of these tries. Then the Saints waked up again and rushed to the other end, where Wagstaffe, under pressure, had to fling the ball back to Holland, who was unable to reach it before Myers got up, and with the line at his mercy he dropped the ball, and Moorhouse made it dead at the expense of a scrummage outside. Huddersfield cleared this and went away with a rush up the left.

Moorhouse was stopped at the 25 line, but the ball was kept in the Saints' quarter and Rosenfeld had hard lines in being denied a score after dribbling over and just letting the ball cross the dead line. Half-time :—

HUDDERSFIELD		3 5—21
ST. HELENS		0 0—0

The one and only time the Challenge Cup final was played in Oldham saw the Huddersfield "team of all talents", under the captaincy of the legendary Harold Wagstaffe (left), demolish St Helens by 38 points to five on May 1st 1915.

The "Past" team in the Past v Present match played at Watersheddings on January 3rd, 1916.
Back Row: J. Wilkinson, J. Whittle, H. Broome, W. Longworth, J. Wright, A. Smith, F. Wormald, G. Kilner, E. Blomley, O. Isherwood.
Middle Row: G. Tyson, R. L. Thomas, G. H. Holden, A. Lees, A. Kershaw, R. Thompson, S. Williams.
Front Row: G.F. Hutchins, Sam Lees Jnr., Sam Lees Snr., A. Ashworth, T. Sellars.

Half-time breather!
The teams (Oldham in white shirts) take a, no doubt, well-earned rest.

THE STANDARD, SATURDAY, OCTOBER 7, 1916.

OLDHAM CHAMPIONSHIP TEAM

THE OLDHAM CRICKET TEAM (CHAMPIONS OF THE CENTRAL LANCASHIRE LEAGUE, 1916) WITH THE CLUB OFFICIALS
Top Row (left to right): George Townley (scorer), G.W. Smith (groundsman), John Clegg, J.E. Broadbent, John Nield, A. Whitmore, C. Stocks, J.W. Halliwell, A. Maylor, A. Ogden, F. Hadfield.
Second Row: A. Price (umpire), R. Platt, B. Goodman, N. Buckley, A. Rhodes, E.B. Shaw, W. Berry, R. Brindle, R. Thompson, G.H. Rhodes (umpire).
Bottom Row: H. Lees, J. Earp, H.H. Whitehead, C. Ibberson. W.H. Taylor, A. Harrop (president), F.S. Holt (captain), J.R. Lawton, C. Beever and P. Taylor.

CENTRAL LANCASHIRE CRICKET LEAGUE

FINAL TABLE

	P.	W.	L.	D.	Pts.
OLDHAM	22	15	4	3	48
MOORSIDE	22	13	5	4	43
CROMPTON	22	12	5	5	41
ROYTON	22	13	7	2	41
LITTLEBOROUGH	22	11	7	4	37
WERNETH	22	7	6	9	30
MIDDLETON	22	8	11	3	27
HEYWOOD	22	6	10	6	24
ROCHDALE	22	6	12	4	22
MILNROW	22	5	11	6	21
WALSDEN	22	5	11	6	21
CASTLETON MOOR	22	4	16	2	14

CRICKET NOTES

CENTRAL LANCASHIRE LEAGUE

CHAMPIONSHIP WON BY OLDHAM

Oldham won the Central Lancashire Cup on Saturday by beating Moorside at Watersheddings, and spice was added to the achievement inasmuch as they wrested the cup from their victims. Oldham

OLDHAM CRICKET CLUB

AVERAGES FOR SEASON 1916.

Matches played 23; won 16, lost 4, drawn 3.
Runs scored for Oldham, 2,930 for 190 wickets; average, 15.04 runs per wicket.
Runs scored for opponents, 1,639 for 208 wickets; average, 7.87 runs per wicket.

BATTING.

	No. of in'gs.	Times not out.	Highest score.	Total runs.	Avge.
H. Goodman	19	2	100*	508	29.88
A. Rhodes	12	0	119	255	21.25
H. Brindle	16	2	82	292	20.86
N. Buckley	18	4	55	251	17.92
G. Potter	8	0	38	138	6.83
E. B. Shaw	21	2	44	300	15.79
C. S. Ibberson	10	0	43	131	13.10
F. S. Holt	22	2	30*	254	12.70
R. Lawton	18	2	53	191	11.98
H. H. Whitehead	14	8	24*	69	11.50
H. Lees	12	0	25	88	7.33
P. Taylor	6	0	17	44	7.33
J. Earp	12	3	17*	62	6.88
W. Terry	7	1	8	23	3.83

Also batted: B. Schofield, 47*, 3, 17, 5*; B. Hampshire, 9, 12, 27*; C. Beeve, 4, 6, 5, 0, 9.
* Signifies not out.

BOWLING.

	Overs.	Mdns.	Runs.	Wkts.	Avge.
H. H. Whitehead	350	85	612	125	4.89
A. Rhodes	127	25	291	31	9.38
J. Earp	110.4	26	357	35	10.28
W. Ler	68	12	198	11	18.00
G. Potter	31	6	62		
H. Lees	28	2	78	4	

FRANK HOLT — THE OLDHAM CAPTAIN

HADYN WHITEHEAD, Oldham's "pro."

1917

Just some of the Oldham players who fought in the First World War.
Top: F. Wise, E.A. Anlezark, T. Brice, G. Cook, J. Owens.
Bottom: R. Marlor, V. Farnsworth, C. Waye, H. Hilton, C. Robeson.

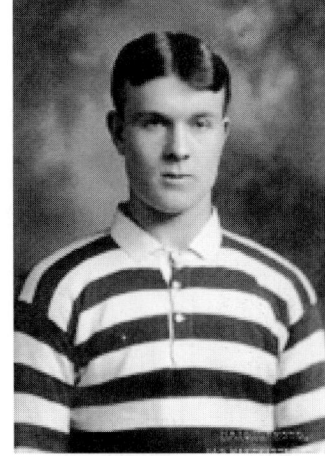

Jim Parkinson, here mentioned in the wounded list on the Army "Roll of Honour" printed in October 1918, played with Hunslet and Coventry as well as the Roughyeds, whom he went on to serve for many years as an official when his playing days were over.

His name can be seen at the bottom of the list.

OBER 24, 1918.

Roll of Honour

THE ARMY

Wounded.

ROYAL ARTILLERY.

ROYAL FIELD ARTILLERY.

BELL, 2 Lt. K. P.
BROWN, Capt. A. V.
BURGESS, Lt. G. H.
DEANE, 2 Lt. W. W.
GIBBS, 2 Lt. F. C.
GREIG, Capt. C. L., M.C
HALLAM, 2 Lt. G. H.
IRONSIDE, 2 Lt. A. S., att T.M.B.
KIRKMAN, Maj. S. C.
LUCAS, Maj. J. de B. T., M.C.
MARKS, 2 Lt. J. M.
PAGNAM, 2 Lt. R. F., att T.M.B.
ROBINSON, Lt.-Col.T. A. F.
WHATTON, Maj. S. M. de H., M.C.

ROYAL GARRISON ARTILLERY

BISHOP, 2 Lt. G. S.
BRISTOL, Lt. E.
CLARK, 2 Lt. H.
FLACK, 2 Lt. W. H.
WOODBURN, Capt. D. B.

ROYAL FUSILIERS.

BOYLE, 2 Lt. J. L.
CROSBY, 2 Lt. H. C.
DAVIE, 2 Lt. J. C.
EVANS, 2 Lt. G. S.
PARKER, 2 Lt. E. W., M.C.
ROGERS, 2 Lt. J. F.
WARD, 2 Lt. E. E.

WORCESTERSHIRE REGIMENT.

GUNDRY, Lt. W. S.
HALES, 2 Lt. G.
HAWTREY, Lt. R. J. C. W.
SMITH, Capt. G. H.
WILES, Lt. F. W.

SOUTH STAFFORDSHIRE REGIMENT.

BEECH, 2 Lt. F. C.
BLUNT, 2 Lt. J. V.
DICKSON, Capt. N. R., M.C.
HOLLOWAY, 2 Lt. C. E.
MUSGROVE, 2 Lt. A. J.
PEARSON, 2 Lt. L.
WATERS, 2 Lt. H. G.

MANCHESTER REGIMENT.

FAZACKERLEY, 2 Lt. J.
FOY, 2 Lt. J. F.
HALLIDAY, 2 Lt. R.
PARKINSON, 2 Lt. J. S.
SMYLIE, Maj. J. S.
TAYLOR, Capt. F. T., M.C
TURNER, 2 Lt. F.

1919

1919 Lancashire Cup winners.

Back Row: *F. Pearce, G.F. Hutchins, J. Blunn, E.A. Anlezark, A. Lees, T. Potter, W.H. Greaves, J.W. Wroe, T. Tetlow, A.E. Tetlow.*
Second Row: *J. Wild, J. Oakes, A.J. Swann (sec.), R. Wylie,* **J. Collins, W. Biggs, W. Thomas, A.E. Moore, H. Carter, E. Davies,** *C. Hutchins,*
J. Finnerty, *H. Langton, F. Howarth.*
Seated: *A. Harrop,* **H. Hilton, W. Hall, J. Ferguson,** *G.W. Holden (pres.),* **D. Holland, J.S. Parkinson, T. Fitton,** *R. Thompson.*
Front Row: D. Thompson, M. Tighe.   *(Players in* **bold** *print)*

OLDHAM FOOTBALL CLUB

EUROPEAN WAR, 1914~1919.

ROLL OF HONOUR

Lt. Col. W. PATTERSON J.P. ✕ Lt. Col. J. B. RYE.

FALLEN IN ACTION:

T. O. JONES	D. SHANNON	A. D. WEST
H. C. MILLS	J. SCOTT	T. WAINMAN

DIED:

W. B. JARDINE

E. A. ANLEZARK	D. FORT	J. S. PARKINSON
J. J. ALLCOCK	D. HOLLAND	C. ROBESON
W. BIGGS	H. HILTON	F. SPEED
T. H. BRICE	P. HEALEY	A. J. SWANN
G. COOK	T. LLEWELLYN	W. THOMAS
H. CARTER	G. LIVERSEDGE	J. TETLOW
W. DIXON Jnr.	J. MARSDEN	R. E. WYLIE
G. B. EVANS	R. MARLOR	T. WHITE
W. FARNSWORTH	E. OLIVER	T. J. WILLIAMS
V. FARNSWORTH	J. OWENS	J. WILTSHIRE
J. FERGUSON		C. G. WAYE
J. FINNERTY		F. W. WISE

Unveiled by the President, G.W. Holden Esq. June 26th, 1920.

MEMORIES OF THE GREAT WAR

A montage of images pertaining to Oldham players in the "Great War" which appeared in the Green Final sports edition of the Oldham Chronicle.

Also the impressive club "Roll of Honour", which was unveiled in the pavilion by club president G.W. Holden on June 26th, 1920. This magnificent memorial was restored thanks to the efforts of local enthusiast Eddie Wolstencroft in 1995.

1920

TOUR REPRESENTATIVES

Evan Davies

*Welshman, Davies was injured
early in the tour but recovered to
force his way into the team for all
three tests in New Zealand.*

Alf Wood

*Wood toured for the second
time in 1920 at the age of 36
and remains the oldest player
ever to do so.*

Herman Hilton

*A local man originally from
the Healey Street amateur
club, Hilton played in all six
tests on the tour.*

IMPRESSIONS OF OLDHAM C.C.

Ralph Whitehead

Bob Shore

A.E. Kershaw

Nornam Brierley

Impressions of some of the players of Oldham Cricket Club, as they appeared in the Green Final in July 1920.

"Excuse me, sir! but you're stood on my ear."

"Nevermind! It's for a good cause."

Mingle Pleasure With Charity and Help the OL— M ROYAL INFIRMARY by going to Watch the Football Match organised by the Oldham Rugby Union Football Club

MANCHESTER & DISTRICT

Mr. Fold's (of Cheshire County) Team v.

OLDHAM RUGBY UNION

AT WATERSHEDDINGS.

TUESDAY, APRIL 19TH, 1921.

Kick Off 6.15 p.m.   Admission 6d. to 5.-

The proceeds, without any deductions whatever, will be given to the Oldham Royal Infirmary.

An advert for a rugby union match held at Watersheddings in aid of the Oldham Royal Infirmary on April 19th 1921.

The following month the "Infirmary Cup", later to become known as the Law Cup, was contested for the first time after being donated for competition between the Oldham and Rochdale clubs by the Rochdale M.P., the Right Hon. A.J. Law.

The first match, played at Rochdale on May 7th, ended scoreless leading to a replay which Oldham won by twelve points to two at Watersheddings on May 13th.

Left: Joe Ferguson, the first captain to raise aloft the Infirmary (Law) Cup in 1921 and this in his twenty second year as a player with the club.

Right: Reg Farrar who set the club record for tries in a season (49) in the 1921-22 campaign.

Both were try scorers in the first Law Cup victory.

OLDHAM'S CHAMPION BOWLER

George Tyson Wins the "Green Final" Challenge Cup

HIGHLY SUCCESSFUL COMPETITION

Oldham's ex international winger George Tyson, here being lauded for his bowling prowess after winning the "Green Final" bowling championship in July 1922.

The paper headline alludes to the fact that George was "mine host" at the Farmers Boy public house on Huddersfield Road at the time.

(right) George pictured on international duty during his rugby playing days.

1922

September 9th 1922. Only the second time the Infirmaries (Law) Cup was contested. The Oldham line up which triumphed 12 - 8 at Watersheddings.
Back Row: *Mr. A.J. Swann (sec.), Joe Ferguson, Alf Tomkins, Sid Rix, Reg Farrar, Bob Sloman, Fred Brown, Jack Collins, Mr. H Langton (pres.).*
Front Row: *Ernie Knapman, Jim Finnerty, Maurice Tighe, Herman Hilton, Alf Bates, Billy Hall, Ned Thomas.*

Oldham "A" team season 1922-23
Back Row: *Higgins, Crowther, Hesketh, Slater, Rees Carruthers, Donovan,*
Front Row: *Collins, May, Hamer, Carter, Hurtley, Grimes.*

8.—THE GREEN FINAL, SATURDAY, DECEMBER 8, 1923.

Some Personalities at the County Match

The "one and only Harold Wagstaff

Billy Batten.

Brough "solid substantial & thick.

Smiler Owen

Tranter, a much prettier player than he looks

Jack Price

Impressions of the county match at Watersheddings by the Chronicle cartoonist "ASM".

Opposite, we see the players who were expected to make most impact on the game. These images were printed in the December 8th 1923 edition, this being the day of the match.

On this page, printed the following week, we see some of the noted attendees and also pick up on the fact that victory went to Lancashire. The red rose county scraped home by six points to five.

SATURDAY, DECEMBER 15, 1923.

The County Match at Watersheddings

BILLY FARNSWORTH signed for Oldham after the 1911 Australian tour of Great Britain along with his brother Vivian. As well as being an international rugby league player he was also an accomplished cricketer, serving as the professional for Oldham Cricket Club and making one appearance for Lancashire C.C.C. against Australia in 1919 at Old Trafford.

BON VOYAGE
"Billy" said goodbye to the Oldham sporting circles and returned to Australia in 1924.

TOUR REPRESENTATIVES

*Oldham had four players on the 1924 tour.
Second-row forward Bob Sloman, full-back Ernie Knapman,
centre or winger Sid Rix and utility player Albert Brough,
who usually played in the forwards but was occasionally
called upon to play in the three-quarters or at full-back.*

A. BROUGH   E. H. KNAPMAN   R. SLOMAN   S. RIX

AUSTRALASIAN TOURISTS, 1924

1924

A SEASON WHEN OLDHAM C.C. WERE UNFORTUNATE NOT TO BRING A TROPHY TO THE OLD 'SHEDDINGS GROUND, WAS 1924, WHEN POPULAR AND ABLE **RALPH WHITEHEAD** WAS PRO. A PRODUCT OF ASHTON-U-LYNE, HE PLAYED FOR THE LOCAL 2ND XI WHEN 14, AND BEFORE HE WAS 17 HAD BECOME PRO FOR KNIGHTON (RADNORSHIRE). SPELLS WITH GRIMSBY, WEST DERBY, ENFIELD, ASHTON, LANCS.C.C.C. (7 SEASONS), GREAT HORTON & WINDHILL FOLLOWED, BESIDES WAR SERVICE, AND ONE SEASON (1919) AT OLDHAM. IN 1924 HE RETURNED TO JOIN F.S.HOLT, P.COOPER, HEBER PLATT, E STARKIE, J.THORPE, B.WALKER, G.FAWLEY, Z.CHESTER, S.WHITTLE, F.THORPE, HAROLD PLATT AND H.MILLS IN A GALLANT BID FOR HONOURS. WOOD CUP SEMI-FINAL-ISTS, DEFEATED BY ROCHDALE, THEY HELD OFF A STRONG CHAMPIONSHIP CHALLENGE BY WERNETH, ONLY FOR ROCHDALE TO CLIMB FROM HALF-WAY, FORCE A TIE AND WIN THE PLAY-OFF. OLDHAM RELEASED WHITEHEAD FOR AN APPOINTMENT AT EAST LANCASHIRE. MASON

C.L.L

George Fawley

Zadok Chester

Stanley Whittle

Harold Platt

Action from the match against Halifax on September 27th 1924. A Halifax player gets a kick away under pressure from Evan Davies. Other Oldham players are, on the left, Tommy Hurtley, and Joe Corsi behind Davies.

More packed terraces for the visit of Barrow on October 11th 1924.
Joe Corsi and Ben Beynon bring down a Barrow player.
Result: Oldham 27 Barrow 5.

Bob Sloman hands off a Rochdale defender in the match on October 25th 1924. Other Oldham players from left to right: Albert Brough, Ambrose Baker, George Hesketh, Jim Fisher (grounded), Evan Davies and Joe Corsi. Over 20,000 spectators gathered at Watersheddings for this Lancashire Cup 1st round match which Oldham won by eleven points to five.

Oldham full-back Ernie Knapman takes a "big-hit" from a Wigan
opponent, but not before releasing a pin-point pass to Sid Rix.
Action from Oldham v Wigan at Watersheddings on December 6th 1924.
Result: Oldham 6 Wigan 0.

A posse of Oldham defenders bundle a Widnes player into touch in the match at Watersheddings on February 21st 1925. Result: Oldham 16 Widnes 2.

Challenge Cup action against Warrington on February 28th 1925. Evan Davies takes on the "Wire" defence with Joe Corsi and George Hesketh in support. Result: Oldham 12 Warrington 2.

Healey Street - Standard Cup winners 1925.

Third from the right on the second row is Thomas Steele, who, during the First World War, received the Victoria Cross, the world's most distinguished honour awarded for bravery.

1925

OFFICIALS AND PLAYERS

Back Row--*Left to Right*   F Pearce F Rixson W Dixon, *Asst Trainer*   A Lees R E. Wylie W Hargreaves
W H Greaves, R L. Thomas, G F Hutchins, T. Taylor F Mills, J S Parkinson A. E Tetlow   Marsden, *Trainer*
F Howarth *Asst Trainer*

Third Row   R Marlor S Rix P Carter J Collins R. Sloman A. Baker G W Holden A Brough R. Thompson
E. H Knapman, C Hutchins, H Langton   Second Row   A. Tomkins J A. Corsi A Woodward G Hesketh
W McCutcheon *President* H Hilton *Captain* E Davies R B Farrar W E. Hall.
Front Row   J Fisher B Beynon, H J Comm T Hurtley

94

COMMITTEE. 1925-26

Back Row   G. F Hutchins, F Rixson R. L. Thomas, R. Thompson G. H. Rhodes, G. W Holden.
Second Row   A. E. Tetlow J S Parkinson W Hargreaves, W McCutcheon *(President)* R. E. Wylie *(Secretary)*
A. H Groves, C Hutchins   Front Row   F. Mills, H. Summerscales, H Langton A. Lees.

SITTING PRETTY!
R.L. Thomas and Arthur Lees, ex-players & club officials.
Both played in the Challenge Cup final in 1899, when Hunslet were defeated 19 - 9.
Arthur Lees was the captain of the Oldham team.

The two images here and others in the 1920s section are taken from a special Oldham F.C. "blotter" book which was issued to celebrate the club's success in the 1925 Challenge Cup.

Above: Trainer Charlie Marsden.
Left: A view of the Hutchins stand complete with asbestos advertisement!

The idea of sporting celebrities sponsoring particular products was in evidence back in the 1920s. The example here shows Herman Hilton and Charlie Marsden extolling the qualities of "Restora" port and sherry available from the T. Lees wine merchants on Ripponden Rd.

"THE WINES OF DISTINCTION"

If you want a bottle of Genuine Wine ask for

FINE OLD **"RESTORA"** (REGD.) **PORT**

The Finest Produce of the Upper Douro District of Portugal

OF GREAT AGE

"Ha!, this is the Port" **"RESTORA"**

FINE OLD **"RESTORA"** (REGD.) **SHERRY**

From the Finest Vineyards of Xerez District of Spain.

OF GREAT AGE

SOLD AT ALL THE LEADING HOTELS

Read the following Testimonial

Sir

On behalf of my colleagues and myself, allow me to compliment you upon the excellence of your "Restora" Port and "Restora" Sherry During our special training for the Rugby League Challenge Cup, which we had the pleasure of winning in Season 1924-25, we found both Wines an excellent tonic, the Port being remarkably light, yet having splendid recuperative qualities.

After a strenuous game or stiff training exercise, the port always proved exceedingly refreshing and any semblance of fatigue was quickly dispelled. We are not desirous of anything better to aid us in our training than the two excellent Wines supplied by you, and in closing we would like to state that you may make whatever use you wish of this communication.

On behalf of the Oldham Football Team.

HERMAN HILTON, Captain.   CHARLES MARSDEN, Trainer

Sole Proprietor **T. LEES,** Wine Merchant, **Ripponden Road, Oldham**

OLDHAM FOOTBALL GROUND

W McCutcheon
PRESIDENT
1924-25—25-26

International Honours
for Wales

1891-2-3 v Scotland
1892-3-4 v England
1893 v Ireland

As he is

As he was

Sam Ogden
Watersheddings' groundsman.

Tommy Hurtley (13) brings down a Rochdale player in the match against Hornets on April 24th 1926.
Other Oldham players left to right: Jack Read, Reg Jones, Rod Marlor, Albert Brough and Jack Collins.
Result: Oldham 26 Rochdale 9.

Percy Carter and Jack Read tackle a Barrow player as Ambrose Baker, Ivor Jeramiah and Joe Corsi watch on.
Action from the match at Watersheddings on October 2nd 1926.
Result: Oldham 27 Barrow 5.

The Pilgrimage to Watersheddings

So dear ol' pals
jolly ol' pals
Sticky together
Thro' all sorts
of weather

Old Sol brightened our
Pilgrimage up to Watersheddings
last Saturday wher the
wicket was in it's usual
sodden state, which makes it such a useful pal to Hartley the slow bowler

It's quite a pleasant
change to draw
Frank Holt with
all his wickets
erect. He kept
them so for
almost match
winning time.

When cricket is slow one can always
go on the roof and play good draughts

The kind-hearted committee
allow some people to see the
match for nothing. To add to
their enjoyment last Saturday
they were provided with a
dog-fight and a run-away horse.

Mr. Holt's strokes are / his leg-guards.
very varied, so are

Gymnastics tableau at Oldham Scholars' Sports at Watersheddings on Tuesday 31st May 1927.

Fred Hartley
Oldham professional 1926 & 1927
Left arm bowler who took 188 wickets.

G. Goddard
Oldham's exciting new young
batting discovery.

James Sharples
Top order batsman who served the
club for almost twenty years.

In the 1927-28 season Swinton won all four domestic trophies; the Lancashire Cup, Lancashire League, Rugby League Challenge Cup and Rugby League Championship. The latter, after a victory over Featherstone by eleven points to nil in the final at Watersheddings on May 5th 1928.

Northern Rugby League — Final Tie.

Featherstone Rovers
:: v. Swinton ::

AT WATERSHEDDINGS, OLDHAM
On Saturday May 5th, 1928.

:: PAVILION TEA TICKET. ::

THE FINAL AT WATERSHEDDINGS

You mon be strong but remember the meek.

The Rev. Chambers preached his farewell sermon last Saturday, and his collection was the ball.

His "welcome". Strong shook hands with him after the match.

Hallsall Swinton's captain.

Bob Sloman, the Oldham forward who played
in all three Ashes winning test matches against
Australia during the 1928 tour and also played
in four consecutive Challenge Cup finals for
Oldham between 1924 and 1927.

Sloman also toured Australia and New Zealand
in 1924.

Ambrose Baker, the Roughyeds' forward,
represented Wales both at union and league.

Emlyn Watkins, Oldham's loose-forward
and former Welsh RU international. He
represented Other Nationalities at rugby
league.

LOCKETT'S FEAT

Takes All Ten Wickets at Royton

Saturday was an ideal day for cricket and the glorious sunshine was naturally an incentive to hoping for the luck of the toss and batting first on good wickets. Although there were many good individual scores, including the second League century of the season, this time by R. W. Murray, of Middleton, it could not be said that the bowlers were without their share of glory.

For A. Lockett, Oldham's popular professional, it was a real joy day, as he took all the Royton wickets for 53 runs, bagging the last eight for 10 runs. He did not do so well at the first, because of the steady batting of G. Horton (34), professional Rushton (28), the skipper H. Hasty (30), and the evergreen J. W. Jones (26 not out), but once he got going he wound up the innings in sensational style. Coming on top of his masterly performance on Friday when he took 8 for 22, includng the "hat trick" against Ashton, it emphasises his wonderful form.

The ball with which he performed his Saturday's feat is to be inscribed and presented to him.

In reply to the home side's 151, Oldham replied with 156 for eight. The best feature of some steady batting was the innings of S. Holt, who missed the coveted half century by but five runs.

Aaron Lockett, the Oldham professional, bagged all ten wickets for 53 runs.

ROYTON v. OLDHAM.

At Royton.

ROYTON

G. Horton b Lockett	34
A. Helliwell c Thorpe b Lockett	20
F. Rushton b Lockett	28
H. Hasty b Lockett	30
J. W. Jones not out	26
A. Taylor b Lockett	1
H. Goodman b Lockett	0
S. Dransfield b Lockett	2
W. Leach lbw b Lockett	4
D. Longbottom b Lockett	0
J. Mavall c and b Lockett	0
Extras	6
Total	151

OLDHAM.

E. Starkie c Hasty b Goodwin	18
R. E. Kershaw c Horton b Rushton	16
H. Platt c Rushton b Goodwin	2
F. L. Collier b Dransfield	14
Lockett b Goodwin	0
S. Holt c Taylor b Rushton	45
J. Thorpe b Goodwin	20
S. Whittle not out	16
J. Hallas run out	1
T. Warrener not out	10
Extras	14
Total (for 8 wkts.)	156

Nº 1737

OLDHAM FOOTBALL CLUB

Sid Rix's Benefit

OLDHAM
v
HULL

AT WATERSHEDDINGS,

Saturday, March 21st, 1931.

Kick-off 3-30 p.m.   Tickets 1/- Each

Photo by J. Edwards, Oldham.

*The home fixture against Hull on March 21st 1931 was set aside as a benefit for Sid Rix.
In twelve years at Watersheddings Sid scored 155 tries, played in the four consecutive Challenge
Cup finals from 1924 to 1927 and went on the 1924 tour to Australia and New Zealand.
He finished his Roughyeds' career with 330 senior appearances.*

Joe Ferguson - The all time leading appearance maker for Oldham with 627, he went on to be the steward at the pavilion and, as these images show, was also a keen bowler.

Here he is seen on the green and outside the bowling pavilion at Watersheddings.

RUGBY LEAGUE CHALLENGE CUP.—1st Round.

RESERVED ENCLOSURE SEAT.
(PAVILION SIDE.)

Block **A** . Row **D** . Seat No. **11**

OLDHAM v. WIDNES

AT WATERSHEDDINGS, OLDHAM,

Saturday, February 7th, 1931.

KICK-OFF 3-30 p.m.

Reserved Seat
3/-
(Including Tax),

R. E. Wylie

SECY.

J. Allan Hanson & Son Ltd., Printers, Oldham.

Rugby League Challenge Cup.—1st Round.
Saturday, February 7th, 1931.
ADMIT TO GROUND.

*Match ticket from the first round Challenge Cup tie against Widnes.
Oldham triumphed by twenty points to five.*

*An interesting presentation at the local Colosseum theatre in
August 1931 with film of both the Roughyeds and the 'Latics
in training at Watersheddings and Boundary Park.*

*The theatre proprietor Mr. W. Cedric Bailey shot the film.
Does any of the footage still exist?*

OLDHAMS POPULAR
COLOSSEUM

THE SUPER "TALKIE"
THEATRE.

Sole Proprietor: W. CEDRIC BAILEY.   Tel. Main 4203.

CONTINUOUS PERFORMANCE DAILY (Saturday excepted) 2 to 11p.m.
SATURDAY .... 2.0, 4.0, 6.30 and 8.40 p.m.

MONDAY, AUGUST 24th, FOR ONE WEEK.
THE MOST DISCUSSED FILM BEFORE THE PUBLIC.

OUTWARD BOUND

(ADULTS ONLY)

Starring DOUGLAS FAIRBANKS, Junr. and HELEN CHANDLER

A Story of a Couple who Wanting to Find Love and happiness in Heaven -
Defied Hell.

Mr. W. CEDRIC BAILEY WILL PRESENT ANOTHER LOCAL FILM
TAKEN UNDER HIS PERSONAL SUPERVISION,

Oldham Football Club Players
AND THE
Oldham Athletic Players

At their Training Quarters, Watersheddings and Boundary Park.
A MOST INTERESTING SPORTING FILM.

COMEDY, SOUND NEWS and INTEREST FILMS.

COMING SHORTLY, THE GREATEST THRILLER OF THE YEAR.

"DRACULA"

Booking Office Open 10 to 10.

Right: A ticket for a whist drive held at Hill Stores on Huddersfield Road to celebrate Oldham official George Hutchins being selected to manage the 1932 tour to Australia and New Zealand.

Note the stewards, Oldham players pictured below, Jack Stephens, Fred Ashworth and Tommy Rees.

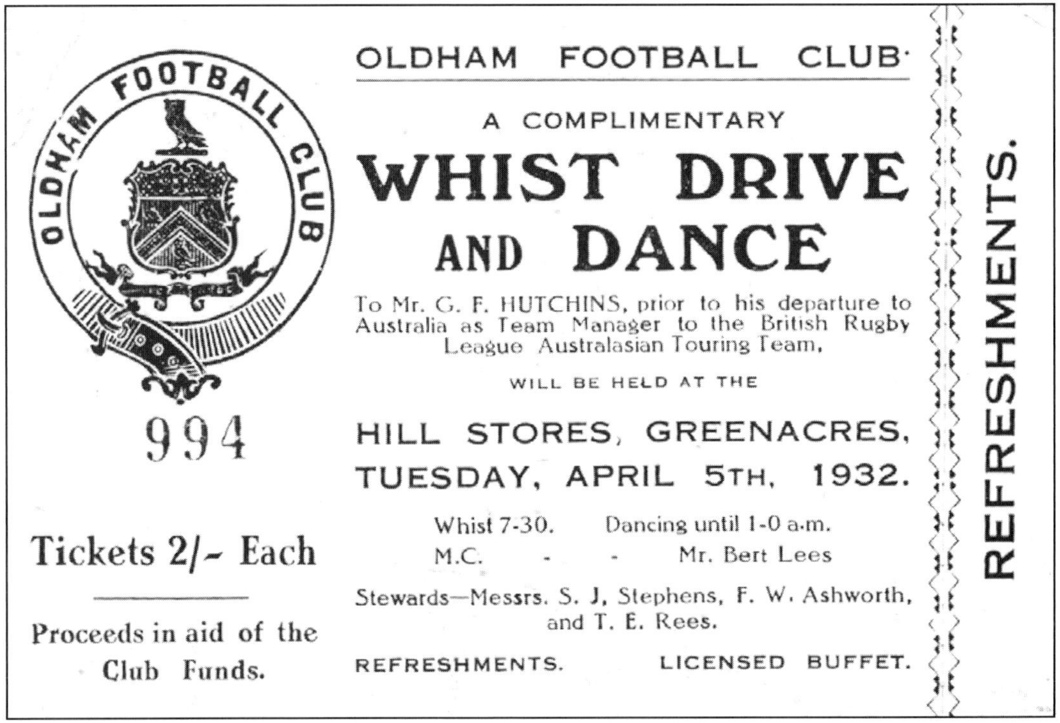

OLDHAM FOOTBALL CLUB·

A COMPLIMENTARY

WHIST DRIVE AND DANCE

To Mr. G. F. HUTCHINS, prior to his departure to Australia as Team Manager to the British Rugby League Australasian Touring Team,

WILL BE HELD AT THE

HILL STORES, GREENACRES, TUESDAY, APRIL 5TH, 1932.

Whist 7-30.   Dancing until 1-0 a.m.
M.C.   -   -   Mr. Bert Lees

Stewards—Messrs. S. J. Stephens, F. W. Ashworth, and T. E. Rees.

REFRESHMENTS.   LICENSED BUFFET.

REFRESHMENTS.

OLDHAM FOOTBALL CLUB

994

Tickets 2/- Each

Proceeds in aid of the Club Funds.

1932

Although Oldham had no players selected for the 1932 tour to Australia and New Zealand, George Hutchins (right) was the co-manager.

He is seen in the group below seated on the extreme right.

The photograph, taken prior to the first test at the Sydney Cricket Ground on June 6th 1932, shows the Australian and Great Britain teams along with the tour managers and some representatives from the first Australian tour to England in 1908.

E.Norman (N.S.W) E.McMillan (N.S.W) J.Wilson (Qld) W.Prigg (N.S.W) D.Dempsey (Qld) P.Madsen (Qld) H.Steinohrt. (Capt.(Qld)) S.Pearce (N.S.W) C.Pearce (N.S.W) F.Laws (Qld) E.Weissel (N.S.W) J.Little (Qld) H.Gee (Qld)

E.Pollard   S.Smith.   A.Ellaby.   W.Horton.   M.Hodgson.   N.Silcock.   J.Sullivan (Capt)   A.Atkinson.   J.Thompson.   L.White.   J.Feetham   J.Brogden.   B.Evans (V.Capt)

Pioneers of 1907 - R.F.Anderton (Eng.Mgr.)   A.Burdon.   H.Glanville.   R.Graves.   E.Fry.   C.Hedley.   J.J.Giltinan.   H.Messenger.   W.Cann.   E.Courtney.   J.Devereux.   H.C.Hamill.   G.F.Hutchins (Eng.Mgr.)

R.Marble   D.Frawley   L.d'Alpuget   A.Dobbs.

OLDHAM C.C
Uncertainty Concerning the Future

MAY LOOSE THE GROUND

Members of the Oldham Cricket Club remain in considerable doubt as to their future owing to the proposed inauguration of greyhound racing at Watersheddings.

They consider it time they were given some definite information on the matter seeing that the Central Lancashire League of which they are members will very shortly be drawing up their fixtures for next summer and there are the important matters of arrangements with the professional and staff.

The Cricket Club has in the past held their ground on a yearly tenancy from the Oldham Rugby Club, which owns it and it is common knowledge that the committee of the other have received a lucrative offer from a greyhound syndicate to rent the field and that plans are being or have actually been prepared for the construction of a track, stands and other buildings.

Thus it will be seen that the continuance of the Cricket Club which has been in existence for upwards of eighty years is in jeopardy.

1932 and the contrast between the uncertainty regarding the fortunes of the Cricket Club and the optimism over the new greyhound stadium are highlighted in these two newspaper articles.

"DEAR OLD PALS"
Dear old pals, jolly old pals sticking together through all kinds of weather.

GREYHOUND RACING
Agreement Signed With the Oldham F.C.

A private company, of which Mr. William Brown of Rochdale, is the promoter, have agreed with Oldham Football Club to take over the cricket ground at Watersheddings to be made into a greyhound racing track. The necessary agreement has been signed and it is intended to proceed with the work at once. The agreement is for five years, with the option of renewal for a further five and the Football Cub receiving a payment of £1,400. It is expected that about two hundred men will be engaged in the lay out and construction of the ground and the promoters are willing to give preference to the Oldham club's players who are out of work As far as possible local labour will be employed. In addition to the rent that the Football Club will receive their financial position will also be relieved through the unemployed players being no longer a charge on them. It is estimated that the cost of making the site into an ideal greyhound racing centre will be about £5,000.

Watersheddings has been home to the Oldham Cricket Club for the last forty four years after their move from Clarksfield in 1889.

1932

OLDHAM FOOTBALL CLUB SUPPORTERS' CLUB

The Supporters' Club was founded at a meeting held in the Temperance Hall, Horsedge Street, Oldham in June 1932. Club officials were appointed with Mr. Lawton secretary, and Mr. J. H. Cocker as treasurer. Elected onto the committee were Councillor Kenyon and Messrs.
T. Beswick, R. Salton,
G. Harlow, H. Sutcliffe, R. Gartside,
J. W. Frost, A. Boardman, W. Woolam,
T. Bubb, Griffiths, A. Quinn, and
J. Adams.
Messrs. Harold Moran and Harry Street

1d on Ball Receipts. 1932.		£.	s.	d.
Sept 3.	St Helens Rec.	1.	18.	1.
" 10.	Halifax "A".	1.	18.	0.
" 17.	Wakefield.	5.	19.	6.
" 24.	Wigan "A".	2.	2.	0.
" 27.	Rochdale Hornets.	2.	2.	0.
Oct 1.	Widnes.	2.	13.	6.
" 8.	St Helens Rec "A".		10.	2.
" 10.	St Helens Rec Cup replay.	12.	10.	
" 13.	do do.		2.	0.
" 15.	Halifax.	4.	3.	9.
" 22.	Barrow "A".	1.	9.	1.
" 29.	Wigan Highfield.	1.	10.	7.
Nov 5.	L.J.L.Federation.	1.	11.	5.
" 12.	Warrington.	2.	15.	10.
" 19.	Wigan Highfield "A".	1.	14.	6.
" 26.	Hull.	2.	12.	11.
Dec 3.	Wigan Highfield.	1.	10.	7.
" 10.	Hull Kingston Rovers.	1.	13.	8.
" 17.	Widnes "A".	1.	9.	9.
" 24.	St Helens.	3.	3.	0.
" 26.	Swinton.	1.	17.	0.
" 28.	Castleford.	2.	13.	11.
" 31.	Wakefield "A".	1.	2.	11.

Football may be the food and drink in itself to the real enthusiast, but nevertheless there is general appreciation of the refreshment buffets opened by the Supporters' Club at Watersheddings.

The now familiar cry by which followers of the Oldham Rugby Club are asked on match days to flirt with the prospect of winning a rugby ball.

OLDHAM v. HEYWOOD

At Oldham.

HEYWOOD

Greenhalgh lbw b Lockett	14
Taylor c Townson b Lockett	37
Jarrott c Halliwell b Lockett ...	23
Slater c Lawton b Lockett	34
Duffy b Wrigley	6
Leach lbw b Lockett	18
Blundell run out	3
Hammond c and b Lockett ...	1
J. Smith c Townson b Kershaw	10
Needham not out	18
Nuttall c Booth b Lockett	1
Extra	1
Total	166

OLDHAM

Lawton b Blundell	33
Booth c Jarrott b Needham ...	2
Kershaw c Greenhalgh b Slater	6
Lockett c and b Needham	27
Halliwell lbw b Needham	9
Holt lbw b Slater	44
Platt b Nuttall	14
Wrigley b Nuttall	2
Lees c Jarrott b Slater	8
Townson not out	0
Burbridge b Slater	1
Extras	15
Total	161

Aaron Lockett
Oldham Cricket Club professional recorded bowling figures of 7 wickets for 62 runs in what would be the club's last ever match at Watersheddings on August 27th 1932.

Stanley Holt
Oldham Cricket captain top-scored with 44 runs.

1933

A reunion of old players took place on January 3rd 1933 when the assembled group were entertained by His Worship the Mayor, Alderman E. Bardsley, J.P. Here they are pictured outside the Town Hall.

J.G. Moffatt.   T.D. Davies.   T. Sellars.

R.L. Thomas.   R.E. Wylie.   J. Ferguson.

T. Fletcher. H. Ellis.   T. Furness. J.H. Wilkinson.   F. Wormald.

T. Cash. S. Williams. A. Lees.   H. Broome.   A.E. Tetlow. J.S. Parkinson.

A.K. Mayall OBE. I.P. Taylor. Ald. E Bardsley. G.F. Hutchins (pres.) R. Thompson (treas.).

OLDHAM SUPER GREYHOUND STADIUM
☞ GRAND OPENING ☜
TO-NIGHT (FRIDAY, JUNE 9th) at 8 p.m.
LICENSED by and Racing under the Rules of the British Greyhound Track Control Society

TRACK NEWS AND GOSSIP.

The Official Opening of the Oldham Super Greyhound Stadium takes place on Friday, June 9th, at 8-0 p.m.

The Directors have not spared expense in building one of the most up-to-date tracks in the country, for they realise that greyhound racing has such a grip on the public that this fascinating sport, promoted on the right lines and under PROPER control, have decided to satisfy a much-needed want in Oldham.

With this in view they are Licensed by, and will race under, the rules of the BRITISH GREYHOUND CONTROL SOCIETY.

The aim of the Oldham Stadium Management is to supply the best possible quality of sport for their patrons, and variety will be their key-note. Patrons of the Oldham Stadium will be at all times the first consideration of the Management.

This will be appreciated by the reduction of admission charges to all enclosures compared with those operating on other tracks.

Particularly will the concession of Ladies being admitted at half-price bring forth favourable comment from that station of the fair sex which enjoys greyhound racing as a pleasant diversion from the ordinary routine of life.

The rapid construction of the Stadium has been made possible only by the valuable help of the local authorities, who have given every possible assistance both in a large and small way.

We hope that these gentlemen at some future date will enjoy the sporting and social facilities which the Oldham Stadium offers.

Our kennels are open to inspection to owners and patrons by arrangement with our Racing Manager.

The luxuries associated with the Kennels are not generally associated with a "Dog's Life."

They can, however, be counted among the minor delights at the Oldham Stadium.

Each Trainer has his own kitchen, and these are the last word in cleanliness and up-to-date fittings.

OUTLINE OF A "DOG'S LIFE."

8-30: Breakfast, consisting of specially prepared Brown bread and fresh milk.

Until noon attention by the Veterinary Surgeon, rest and exercise.

4-0 to 4-30: Dinner. This consists of specially prepared Brown bread soaked in broth, also a meat course of lamb's or beast's head and beef, with necessary vegetables.

Fish is included once a week, whilst a special diet is prepared for any sick or ailing dogs in the specially set and Isolation Kennels. Of course, special dieting is the rule when a dog has an engagement to meet during the day.

SAFETY OF DOGS.

There are at present well over one hundred dogs in the kennels, and elaborate precautions are taken for their safety. Watchmen are in attendance throughout the night, and in the event of any disturbance a switch at their disposal immediately floodlights the various bays and kennels. Anyone venturing to tamper with the dogs would have very little chance of escape.

Special transport arrangements have been made, and the racing will be over at 9-30 approx.

Cars and buses pass the ground, and ample parking arrangements are well in hand.

There is covered accommodation for 5,000 people, so we are prepared for all kinds of weather.

Racing every Monday, Wednesday, Friday and Saturday at 8 p.m.

Matinee each Tuesday at 3-15.

Popular Prices: 2/- and 1/- (including tax). Ladies Half-Price.

Come in Your Thousands and See the Most Thrilling Sport of to-day.

Racing Wet or Fine. All Under Cover.

Flat and Hurdle Races.

Driven from Home

OLDHAM C.C.

GONE TO THE DOGS

OLDHAM V? BEENS

G. POTTER
A. SMITH
C. SWAILES
G. RHODES
B. WALKER
J. ARMSTRONG
W. FARNSWORTH
J.R. LAWTON.
C. MILDENHALL
DR. WOOD.
H. HORTON.
J. MILLS.
F.S. HOLT
R. WHITEHEAD.
ETC. ETC.

O.C.C.

Gloomy times for the Cricket Club as the advent of Greyhound racing brought its time at Watersheddings to an end after 44 years of occupation.

S. HOLT - Oldham C.C.

*Oldham Cricket captain,
Stanley Holt, ponders the club's future.*

OLDHAM FOOTBALL CLUB
BASEBALL
At Watersheddings,
On SATURDAY, AUG. 5th, 1933, COMMENCE AT 3 P.M.
1st DIVISION ENGLISH LEAGUE MATCH
CRYSTAL
(League Champions and Robert Mark's Cup Winners) V.
NEW BRIGHTON
(Semi-Finalists, Lewis Cup and E.B.A. Cup);

Also CHALLENGE MATCH--CUMBERLAND v. WESTMORLAND
WRESTLING:
Ex-Guardsman EDWARD HODGSON
(Oldham's New Forward) V.
FERGY SOUTHWARD
(Salford and Cumberland County)

GOAL KICKING COMPETITION
J. HOEY (Widnes).   T. E. REES (Oldham)
W. J. HOLDING (Warrington).   W. GOWERS (Rochdale H.)
F. ADAMS (Halifax).   H. LOCKWOOD (Huddersfield)
(Winner of Leeds R.F.C. Goal Kicking Competition).

CHALLENGE GOAL KICKING COMPETITION
JIMMY LOMAS
(Late Salford and Oldham) V.
BEN GRONOW
(Late Huddersfield and Bradford N.)

The OLDHAM RIFLES BAND will play appropriate Music.

Admission (including Tax) Ground & Side Stands 1/-, Seats 6d. extra, Unemployed 6d.
(Upon Production of Unemployment Card).

*A grand day out at Watersheddings with the main event baseball match being supplemented by a wrestling bout featuring Oldham's new Cumbrian forward **Ted Hodgson** (above left) and two goal kicking competitions. **Tommy Rees** (above right) represented Oldham against the marksmen from other rugby league clubs and the legendary **Jim Lomas** (below) featured in a special contest against the former Huddersfield great Ben Gronow.*

This photograph, taken during the Oldham v Australia match on September 9th, 1933, shows how the main stand was constructed on a curve so as to accommodate the better viewing of games by the spectators.

Result:
Oldham 6
Australia 38

Aerial view of the Watersheddings site taken circa 1934.

OLDHAM		G. T.	ROCHDALE HORNETS		G T.
1. Rees, T. E. (Capt.)			1. Gowers, W.		
2. Taylor, A.			2. Skillen, A. C.		
3. Bardsley, S.			3. Beattie, G. E.		
4. Givvons, A.			4. Armbruster, L. V. (Capt.)		
5. Lewis, L.			5. Gaunt, R.		
6. Egan, T.			6. Aynsley, C. J.		
7. Reynolds, J. B.			7. Burkill, R.		
8. Read, J.			8. Moaby, A. J.		
9. Scaife, J. M.			9. Lister, R.		
10. Rees, L.			10. Moore, W. J.		
11. Ashworth, F. W.			11. Mills, G. E.		
12. Blossom, F.			12. Walker, B.		
13. Pugh, N.			14. Campbell, M.		
14. Clayton, A.			Sutcliffe, B.		

Referee:— Mr. A. E. Harding, of Broughton.

Oldham Football Club,

WATERSHEDDINGS GROUND.

OLDHAM AND ROCHDALE INFIRMARIES CUP.

Oldham v. Rochdale Hornets

Saturday, August 18th, 1934.

Kick-off 3-30 p.m.

*Oldham full-back Tommy Rees appeared in eleven consecutive
Infirmary Cup matches 1928-38 scoring 33 goals and 1 try.*

Alex Givvons

Jack Read

Jack Scaife

Lew Rees

Norman Pugh

Some of the Oldham players who featured in the Infirmary Cup victory over Rochdale (20 - 7) on August 18th, 1934.

1934

THE CANTEEN LADIES

These ladies will probably be surprised to see their reflection in this "Mirror" to-night. Most visitors to the Oldham Football Club's ground will recognise them as the Canteen Ladies, cheerful winter spirits of Watersheddings.

Here snapped on their annual outing to New Brighton they are from left to right:—Back row: Miss Tetlow, Miss Preston, Miss Harrison and Miss Baker. Front row: Mrs. Sutcliffe, Mrs. Woolam, Mrs. Hunter and Mrs. Hollingworth.

A day out for the Watersheddings canteen ladies.

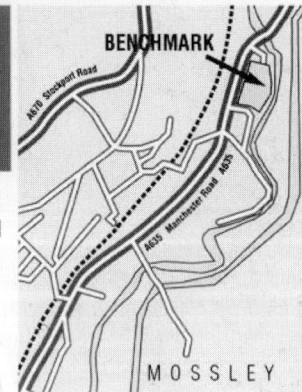

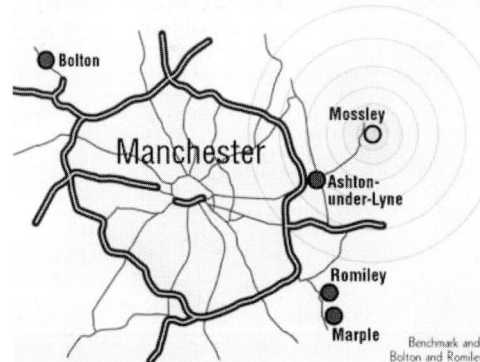

Oldham v Villeneuve

THE STANDARD, FRIDAY, SEPTEMBER 21, 1934.

On September 17th 1934, Oldham played hosts to a French touring team from Villeneuve and although the French gave an entertaining display which won them many friends, the last say went to the Roughyeds.

Full-back Tommy Rees (below) won the match with the last kick of the game, a towering drop goal from out near the touch-line.
Result: Oldham 26 Villeneuve 25.

WE PLAY 'RUGBY A TREIZE'

AYE MON! THA' PLAYS RUGBY A TREAT

THE ELEGANT JEAN GALIA OF SPORTING ATHLETIC VILLENEUVE, WHICH INCLUDES

MONSIEUR 'SAMSON' MOISSET, THIS 'TAWNY' LITTLE WINGMAN DID THE HORIZONTAL LIFT WITH OUR FORWARDS; AND

M. ROUSSE, WHO HAS COVERED A LARGE PART OF ENGLAND SINCE HE ARRIVED.

MAX ROUSIÉ MADE THE GREYHOUNDS HIDE THEIR FACES, AND ASK THEIR KENNEL BOY TO MAKE THEM INTO A FRENCH POODLE!

DESPITE ROUSSE AND ROUSIÉS ROUSING RUNS, REES' 'ROUSE' WON THE DAY. GOOD OL' TOMMY! VIVE LA FRANCE! BISMAN '34

1934

The Oldham team which defeated Bramley (23 – 8) on September 1st 1934 at Watersheddings.
Back Row: Bob Cattlin, Les Lewis, Norman Pugh, Frank Blossom, Ab Clayton, Jack Read, Edgar Brooks, G.W. Smith.
Front Row: Wilf Whitworth, Steve Ray, Alex Givvons, Tommy Rees, Jack Reynolds, Jack Stephens, Fred Ashworth.

The next few years will encompass the baseball phenomenon that occurred at Watersheddings in the 1930s.

Oldham Greyhounds' first official match was the league game played away against Hurst Hawks on 11th May 1935.

Baseball Season Opens at Oldham:

THE weather looked so much like the Friday before an Oldham F.C. home match that I nearly telephoned Watersheddings this morning to get the teams. The thermometer said it was the football season. The calendar said it was the merry month of May, although no doubt the South African cricketers had other words for it.

◆ ◆

However, Oldham's baseball season starts to-morrow, and I do not mean May-be, as our American friends might say. The Greyhounds are ready, the Blue Sox mean business, the diamond is in perfect condition.

◆ ◆

It will be Oldham's first baseball league game and the Greyhounds, as the Stadium team is called, are playing Manchester North End Blue Sox. The match starts at three o'clock.

Game Explained

A BIG crowd is expected, and arrangements have been made for a service of special buses to the Stadium. Many Oldham sportsmen may go up out of curiosity, having had few previous opportunities for watching the game. They will find that baseball is as simple to follow as it is swift in action, and every move in the game will be explained through a loud speaker by an expert.

◆ ◆

The Oldham Greyhound are regarded as one of the strongest teams in the league with their international battery consisting of Raddell, catcher, and Riches, pitcher.

Footballers Play It

AN interesting personal point about to-morrow's game which will appeal to Rugby fans is that on each side will be a famous full-back. Jim Sullivan will play for the Blue Sox and Tom Rees for the Greyhounds.

◆ ◆

Tom Rees is a newcomer to the game but has picked it up quickly enough to get his place in the team, while Sullivan played the English baseball code for some years. Sullivan plays at first base and is a big hitter.

Joe McNally, the Oldham forward, is another Rugby League player who looks like doing well at baseball, and has already shown that he knows how to get his weight behind a big hit.

The Brothers Gaunt

ALSO included in the Greyhounds' team are the Gaunt brothers, Roy and Sid, of Rochdale Hornets, who both know the game, their football colleague, Cecil Aynsley, and Mowat, the Canadian expert.

In addition to Sullivan there is another well-known Rugby player in the Blue Sox side. He is Guy Wilson, the well-known Rugby Unionist. Broadhurst, the former Manchester City centre forward, will play at third base for Blue Sox.

◆ ◆

Both the Greyhounds and the Blue Sox won their opening games last Saturday and a close contest is anticipated.

Diamond Protected

THE diamond at the stadium has been carefully prepared and the recent wet weather has brought it to the peak of condition. It has been protected overnight.

◆ ◆

The teams will be:—Oldham Greyhounds: Catcher, H. Raddall; pitcher, W. Riches; first base, Roy Gaunt; second base, C. Aynsley; third base, Syd Gaunt; short step, Alec Mowat; left field, J. McNally; centre field, Tom Rees; right field, T. Bannon. Benchers (substitutes) I. Jones, M. Wright, M. Downey. Coach, Billy Riches. Manchester North End: Horrocks, Rushby, Jim Sullivan Brooks, Broadhurst, Gregory, Plumpton, Guy Wilson, Rogers.

◆ ◆

The admission prices are one shilling, sixpence, and twopence for boys.

◆ ◆

BASEBALL NOVELTY AT OLDHAM

Oldham Greyhounds put on Early Spurt

Oldham Greyhounds 25, Manchester N. E. Blue Sox 16

The Oldham Greyhounds won their first home match and their second in succession in the National Baseball League at The Stadium, Watersheddings, on Saturday, when they beat Manchester North End Blue Sox by 25 runs to sixteen. In spite of the cold weather there was a crowd of about three thousand who, judging by their applause, took a close in the game and thoroughly enjoyed it. The innings scores were:—

Greyhounds: 1 5 2 0 2 1 0 0 3 2
Blue Sox: ... 2 0 1 0 1 2 1 3 6

It will be observed from the scores that the game was won and lost in the first innings when the Greyhounds put the score board out of action straightaway by hitting up the exceptional total of fifteen runs. For this total they were greatly helped by some powerful hitting by McNally, who twice hit the ball out of the ground for two home runs on each of which he brought a couple of men home with him. The Greyhounds gained more runs by taking full advantage of mistakes in the field. There was some erratic throwing to base and the Blue Sox pitcher, Rushby, bowling at medium pace, was let down by his out-fielders, who dropped three catches in the first innings. Blue Sox were just as nervous at the plate, and made only two runs in response to their opponents' heavy total.

Blue Sox Recover

However, after this sensational start a dramatic change came over the game. Blue Sox made a brilliant recovery. They made their first step towards keeping the Greyhound batters idle by putting Guy Wilson in the pitcher's box. With the wind behind him, Wilson pitched at a great pace and not only kept the score down but had the satisfaction of retiring the Greyhounds on three occasions before they could make a run.

In addition to Wilson's good work, the Blue Sox had a great fielder in Sullivan at first base. In the remaining eight innings the Greyhounds obtained only ten runs from Wilson's pitching, while the Blue Sox became far more confident with the bat. In fact, taking the game as a whole, the visitors seemed to have the more consistent batters and men were coming in very nicely off third base when Tom Rees, with a smart catch in the outfield, ended the last innings with the Blue Sox score at six.

However, if it was the Blue Sox who were more reliable with the bat, it was from the Greyhounds that the crowd got much of the spice of the afternoon. The visitors had a bold stealer of bases in Lapin, but none of them had that mastery of between base trickery that was displayed by Riches, and sometimes by Syd Gaunt. Clearly, Riches is a wit, as full of tricks as any scrum-half and just as interesting to watch whether pitching or running, if running is the word to apply to that nonchalant lope of his from base to base. After watching other batters taking no risks and running furiously the crowd, most of whom, of course, were new to the game, were nonplussed at first by the way in which Riches ambled on to the next base when the ball was in hand. When they got accustomed to him they laughed out loud at his impudence.

It was always exciting to watch Riches midway between two bases turning first to one and then the other as excited fielders threw the ball to and fro over his head and, as often as not, to the great delight of the crowd he bluffed his way to safety.

Brothers do Well

The home team were splendidly served by their catcher, Raddell, and some good picking up and throwing was done at short stop by Mowatt. Syd and Roy Gaunt shared the batting honours with McNally, and each of them had the distinction of hitting a home run.

As a new game to this part of the world baseball must have impressed everyone with its possibilities for all round skill in running, throwing and batting, and for its continuous action and incident.

The teams were.

Oldham Greyhounds: Raddell, Riches (coach), R. Gaunt, Aynsley, S. Gaunt, Mowat, McNally, Rees, Bannon.

Manchester North End Blue Sox: Horrocks, Rushby, Sullivan, Byrom, Broadhurst, Gregory, Plumpton Wilson, Rogers.

SATURDAY, MAY 25, 1935

The New Lodger

John Bull the cricketer: Whose this base guy banging on the door to disturb my peaceful summer ?

"Sure John it's your own 1st cousin come right up to see you some time."

C. AYNSLEY (OLDHAM GREY-HOUNDS)

Cecil Aynsley was an Australian who played for Rochdale Hornets and like many of his rugby league colleagues tried his hand at baseball.

1935

A special celebration held at Watersheddings in May 1935 to commemorate the Silver Jubilee of the reign of His Majesty King George V and Queen Mary.

Top left: Joe Ferguson and family outside the George Hotel specially bedecked with bunting and the union flag to mark the jubilee.

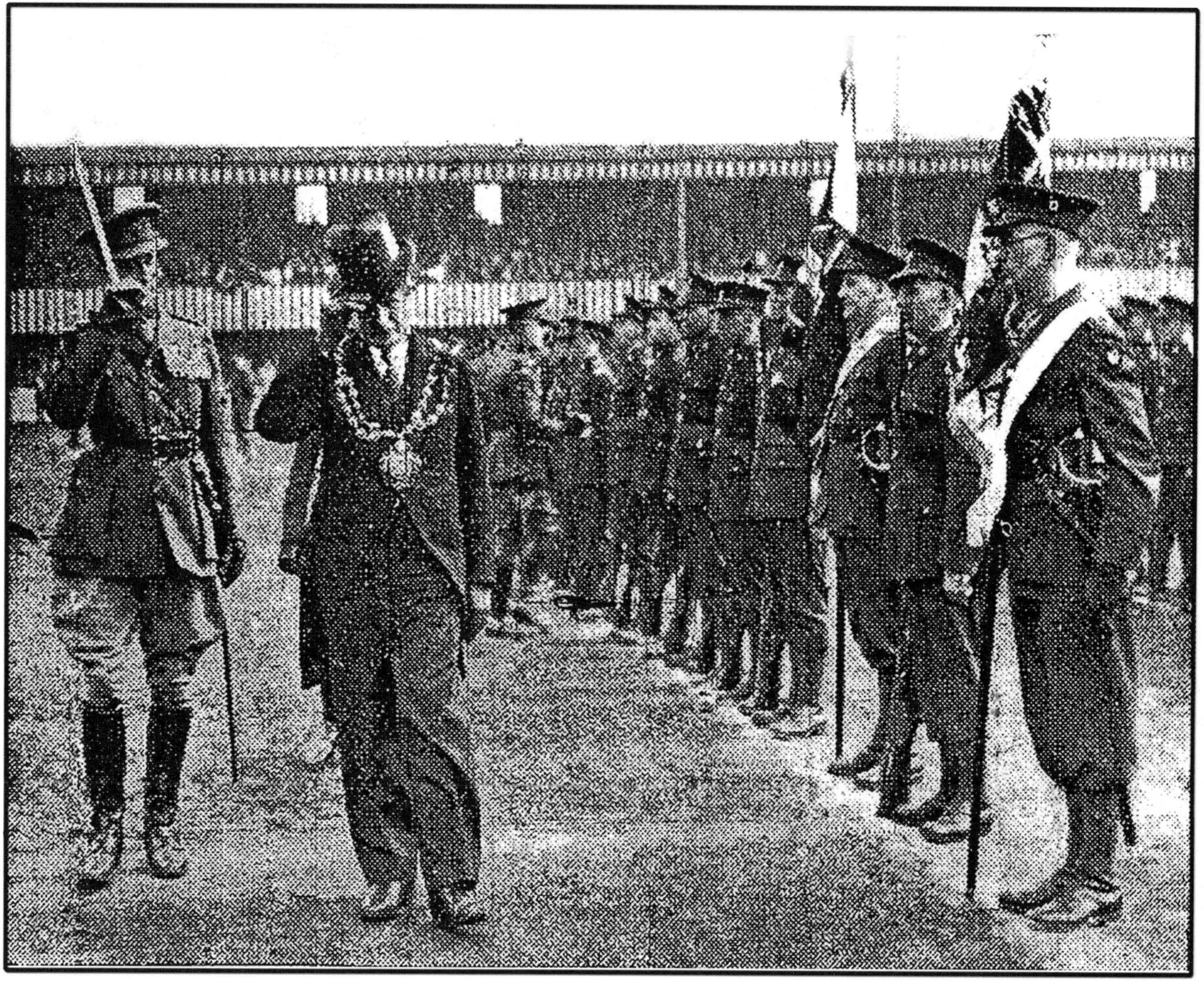

1935

International Women Footballers

International ladies football graced the Watersheddings turf in August 1935 when England took on France.

(England were actually represented by the Dick Kerr team based in Preston.)

TOP DOGS!

BASEBALL CHAMPIONSHIP FOR GREYHOUNDS

REQUIRING only one point to make sure of winning the championship of the North of England National Baseball League, Oldham Greyhounds made no mistake against Hurst Hawks, running out victors by twenty points to nil. The match was noteworthy for the brilliant pitching of Leo Fred, who set up a record by retiring the opposition pointless. There was a record crowd, the Watersheddings folk giving the Greyhounds a fine ovation at the end of the match.

The final positions in the North of England National Baseball League are as follows:—

	P	W	D.	L.	Pts
Oldham Greyh'nds	14	12	1	1	25
Bradford Northern	14	10	2	2	22
Rochdale Greys	14	8	2	4	18
Salford Reds	14	6	2	6	14
Manchester N.E.	14	5	2	7	12
Belle Vue Tigers	14	5	1	8	11
Hurst Hawks	14	3	0	11	6
Hyde Grassh'pers	14	2	0	12	1

Oldham the Top Dogs

"Hangings" at the Stadium

BASEBALL IN THE GLOAMING, AT THE EXHIBITION NIGHT."

EXHIBIT 'A' SHOULD BE THE LONDON LADS DISPLAYING THEIR SHORT PASSING GAME". IT LEFT TOMMY REES GASPING.

BUT HE'S SO ENERGETIC WE COULDN'T FIX HIM IN ONE PICTURE. IF HE MAKES A ONE BASE HIT HE ALMOST BUSTS

ANOTHER WHO SHOULD BE 'HUNG' IS NOT THE UMPIRE, NOR THE WATERHEAD PUNTER, WHO SAID "THEY FAVOUR JOCKIES ONT'NEET TURN,"

BAH!

BUT BARE-LEGGED ZOLA ALBEIT, THE BASE. HE'LL PROBABLY CLEAR THE STAND WHEN HE SCORES A HOME RUN.

BISMAN 35

BASEBALL PLAYER SENT OFF!

Over five thousand spectators witnessed the defeat of Oldham Greyhounds baseball team at Watersheddings in their exhibition match against a London select side. The visitors won by 11 runs to 6 after a most interesting exhibition of catching and base throwing.

The game was marred by some questionable decisions by the umpire, and unfortunately the Oldham catcher was given marching orders half-way through the game for voicing his objections to one of the umpire's decisions.

Higginshaw Epic

The visit of local amateur team Higginshaw in the first round of the Challenge Cup in February 1936 caused much local interest. "Higgy" had the audacity to take the lead with an early penalty goal but Oldham eventually eased home by 38 points to two. However, the amateurs acquitted themselves well and would have taken some comfort and financial reward from the crowd of just under 8,000.

1936

Greenacres R.F.C. 1936
Back Row: F.A. Schofield, G. Pickford, J. Minton, J. Birchall, A. Carter, J. Stott, R. Walker.
Front Row: W. Travers, T. Cross, F. Bird (capt.), M. Taylor, H. Clark, H. Bennett.

138

"Oldham Standard" Cup

JUST A MINUTE FOLKS!

HERE WE ARE BEHIND THE 'STANDARD CUP!'

OH, NO! WE DIDN'T WIN IT. WE WATCHED GREENACRES. THEY DESERVED IT. ANYONE WHO STOPPED A 'HIGGY' FORWARD LAST SATURDAY DESERVED TEN CUPS!

ICE CREAMIO

FLOWER POT

BUT SCHOFIELD, CLARK AND BARBER WOULD HAVE STOPPED BADOGLIO IN A TANK, AND MINTON MIGHT HAVE

STOPPED AN AIR ATTACK; WHEN THEY STOP 'EM AT GREENACRES THEY CERTAINLY STAY STOPPED!

GREENACRES....9 HIGGINSHAW....5

For the second season in succession the Oldham Standard Cup was in the keeping of Greenacres. On this occasion the trophy was gained by victory on the field instead of being awarded to them without a final tie being played as was the case the previous year. Then Higginshaw failed to turn up for the final after a row with the Oldham Supporters' Club over "gate money" regarding the postponing of the final of their Workshop Competition arranged to be played for at Watersheddings on the same night.

Harry Clarke
Greenacres Captain

J. Minton
Greenacres full back

J. Costello
Greenacres
scored a try

Barber
Greenacres

Wintry action from Watersheddings in the 1930s.

Right: Alex Givvons scoops up the ball.

Mr. Leo Dallas Sturgeon, the American consul in Manchester, unfurls the Oldham Greyhounds championship pennant before the start of the 1936 season.

Looking on from left to right are: Mr. W. Brown (Oldham stadium manager), Zola Albert, Leo Fred, Sid Olansky and Mr. John Moores.

Greyhounds' Brilliant Opening

DAZZLING PLAY BY LEO FRED

A fine day marked the opening of the baseball season at Watersheddings, when three thousand people attended to see Oldham Greyhounds, the 1935 champions, play the Rest of the League. The Rest fielded quite a strong side but notable absentees were Jim Sullivan and Bennett, of Wigan, who were playing in the Rugby League semi-final at Hull.

After Mr. Leo Dallas Sturgeon, the U.S. Consul in Manchester, had hoisted the first championship pennant, he was introduced to the successful Oldham team which contained eight players from Canada or the States. Mr. John Moores, president of the N.B.A., presented miniature pennants to the players.

The final positions in the North of England National Baseball League are as follows:—

	P.	W.	D.	L.	Pts
Oldham Greyh'nds	14	12	1	1	25
Bradford Northern	14	10	2	2	22
Rochdale Greys	14	8	2	4	18
Salford Reds	14	6	2	6	14
Manchester N.E.	14	5	2	7	12
Belle Vue Tigers	14	5	1	8	11
Hurst Hawks	14	3	0	11	6
Hyde Grassh'pers	14	2	0	12	1

Mr John Moores, president of the National Baseball Association, presents pennants to the Oldham Greyhounds championship winning team.

The players left to right are: Harry Raddell, Billy Riches and Leo Fred.

OLDHAM GREYHOUNDS WIN LEAGUE CHALLENGE TROPHY

Leo Fred, captain of the Oldham Greyhounds, receives the cup from John Moores, president of the National Baseball Association.
The manager of the "Greyhounds", Mr Fred Brown, is on the left of the photograph.

By defeating Manchester Blue Sox last Saturday Oldham Greyhounds won the North of England Baseball League Challenge Cup. Each player on the winning side received a miniature cup.

Back row: Mr. Langford (N.B.A.), Roy Gaunt, Syd Gaunt, W Hicklin, J. McNally, H. Richardson, Zola Alpert, W. Watts, Mr. W Brown (manager of the Greyhounds).

Front row: Pete Stevenson, W Riches, T. Rees, Mr. J. H. Moores (president N.B.A.), Leo Fred, Mrs. Moores, Scotty Palfrey G. Mellor.

THE STANDARD, THURSDAY, AUGUST 27, 1936

TIMELY CHARITY

EVEN OUR FRIEND THE DOOR-KEEPER WAS MOST CHARITABLE LAST SAT. HE THOUGHT WE WERE FROM THE CLOCKMAKERS UNION.

'OLDHAM 'LAID THEMSELVES OUT' TO BE GOOD HOSTS. MR. PUGH SUPPORTED THE HOSPITALS. IN A SKULL CAP, HE SEEMED TO BE TRYING TO FILL 'EM TOO, UNTIL HE CAME ACROSS SID. GAUNT, WHO ALSO REALISED THAT PREVENTION IS BETTER THAN CURE, EVEN IN A CHARITY MATCH.

OLDHAM STAGGERED HOME WITH GRANDMOTHER CLOCKS, BUT ROCHDALE WILL STILL HAVE TO ASK A BOBBY FOR ANOTHER 12 MONTHS.

WHAT! NO CLOCKS

BISMAN '36.

The 1936 Infirmary Cup saw the winning players awarded "grandmother" clocks.

Here is a cartoon summary of the events. Oldham won by twelve points to four.

Below: Welshman, Ceidriog Davies, who scored two tries in the above mentioned victory over Rochdale.

145

"Standard" Cup Final

FERRANTI'S R.F.C. 28 PTS.
GREENACRES R.F.C. 2 PTS.

IN THIS 'STANDARD CUP' FINAL, THE CHIEF FEATURES WERE QUAIL'S EARLY GOAL FOR GREENACRES, WHICH PUT ALL THE —

FERRANTI LOUD SPEAKERS ON A MUCH LOUDER WAVE-LENGTH; FLYING FLATLEY'S FOUR FINE TRIES;

LES. BAYLIFFE'S GRIN BEHIND A WELL-EARNED CUP;

AND AN IMPROMPTU EXHIBITION BY THE BARROWSHAW RUGBY FOOTBALL STARS.

AN INCIDENT WHICH LED TO THE DISMISSAL

OF A GREENACRES PLAYER LEFT THE LOSERS' SUPPORTERS FEELING VERY DOWN IN THE MOUTH.

Ferranti won the 1937 Standard Cup by beating Greenacres 28 points to 2 to become the cup holders for the first time in the club's history.

J. HARDMAN.

One of the outstanding players for Ferranti.

V. FLATLEY.

Ferranti's dashing right winger who scored four tries in the final.

Oldham Greyhounds Baseball team May 1937.
Back Row: *T. Rees, J. Davey, J. McNally, S. Olansky, K. Robinson, W. Goldstein, A. Baker (trainer).*
Front Row: *W. Hickling, J. Porter, J. Faulkener, L Turner (manager), H. Mercer, T. Michell, C. Holt, H. Cronshaw.*
Sat crossed legged at the front is the mascot (batboy) Bill Pearce.

1937

Another team photo for the Oldham Greyhounds from 1937, this one featuring no less than rugby league legend Gus Risman in the line-up.
Back Row: Gus Risman, Jack Porter, George Shaw, Reg West, Zola Albert, Jack Green, Stapleford, Jim Davey, Sid Olansky, Hallsworth.
Front Row: Bert Shaw, Ken Robinson (capt.), Mr. P. Mitchell, Mr. L. E. Turner (manager), Mr. H. Mercer, Tommy Rees, Harry Radell.   Bat boy: Bill Pearce.

Greyhounds arrive in Oldham from various London tracks to supplement the kennels at the Oldham Stadium at Watersheddings.

MR. E. LANDLESS TURNER, MANAGER OF OLDHAM GREYHOUNDS, HAS BEEN COMBING GLASGOW (AT 4 O' CLOCK IN THE MORNING) FOR TALENT FOR HIS ALL-STAR TEAM.

SAY! CAN YOU PLAY BALL?

MR. TURNER WAS SECRETARY TO THE MANCHESTER COUNTY BASEBALL ASSOCIATION FROM ITS INCEPTION TO THE PRESENT SEASON; WAS TEAM MANAGER TO ENGLAND IN 1935, AFTER HELPING TO FORM THE NORTH OF ENGLAND LEAGUE. HE WAS COMMENTATOR ON THE FIRST COMPLETE GAME BROADCAST IN GREAT BRITAIN. IN HIS SPARE TIME MR. TURNER IS HON. WHIP TO A BEAGLE PACK, AND SO HE EXPECTS THE 'GREYHOUNDS' TO BE IN AT THE KILL, AND MAKE NO BONES ABOUT THE NORTH OF ENGLAND HONOURS.

NOT EVEN A WISH BONE

BISMAN '37

Baseball

OLDHAM WIN THE PENNANT

Caledonians Easy Prey

OLDHAM GREYHOUNDS have added to their annual succession of honours by regaining the North of England League Championship pennant in their third year. In 1935 they won the championship, in 1936 the League Cup and only lost the pennant after a play-off with Rochdale, and now, in 1937, they have had perhaps their most successful season, getting to the semi-final stage of the English Cup, and the final of the League Cup. On top of all this comes the bombshell that there may possibly be no baseball team in Oldham next season, in spite of the fact that the Greyhounds have commanded regular gates of four thousand, and have on occasion approached six thousand.

Fans may be optimistic, however, as I undersand that negotiations are pending for the establishment of a team elsewhere in Oldham next year.

KEN ROBINSON, BOXER & BASEBALL COACH TO THE GREYHOUNDS CERTAINLY KNOWS HOW TO PRODUCE 'STARS' — HE HAS DELIVERED 11 K-Os SINCE COMING TO ENGLAND TWO YEARS AGO. BORN AT KINGSTON, ONTARIO, KEN WAS CANADIAN MIDDLE-WEIGHT AMATEUR CHAMPION, AND COACHED AN ARMY BASEBALL TEAM

HIS FIRST ENGLISH CLUB WAS LITTLEWOOD'S, LIVERPOOL. LAST SEASON ROBINSON WAS COACH TO BELLE VUE TIGERS.

PLAYED FOR THE REST OF ENGLAND v. LONDON IN 1935, AND HELPED LANCS. DEFEAT YORKS. LAST SEASON. HE HAS WON 22 FIGHTS OUT OF 33 IN THIS COUNTRY. YEA! THIS BOY CAN SURE BIFF THE ONION!

GEORGE SHAW, THE MOST POLITE HURLER IN THE NORTH OF ENGLAND LEAGUE, ALWAYS TOUCHES HIS CAP TO PROSPECTIVE VICTIMS.

BEING AN ICE HOCKEY STAR HE'S A COOL CUSTOMER AND GIVES ASPIRING 'SWATTERS' AN ICY WELCOME WITH GURTH, ALSO OF THE GREYHOUNDS, HE HAS ASSISTED STREATHAM ICE HOCKEY CLUB, (CHAMPIONS TWO YEARS AGO), FOR FOUR SEASONS INTERESTED IN WRESTLING, RUNNING, AND FIELD SPORTS

AFTER PLAYING FOR A SENIOR LEAGUE CLUB IN ONTARIO, GEORDIE JOINED THE LONDON WHITE CITY CLUB 'KEEP 'EM DOWN THE ALLEY, GEORGE, AND THE GREYHOUNDS WILL BE SKATING AFTER THAT PENNANT!

BASEBALL
(National Baseball Association Rules)
AT WATERSHEDDINGS
LANCASHIRE v
AMERICA (U.S. OLYMPIC TEAM)
SATURDAY, August 20th at 6-45 p.m.
[Please Note: Pitch-off 6-45 p.m., not 7 p.m. as shown on posters.]
Admission: Ground 1/-, Stand 1/- extra.
Boys Half-Price to Ground only

Ross Kendrick the Oldham Greyhound pitcher was the outstanding player for Great Britain in their 4-1 World Amateur Baseball championship victory against the touring United States Olympic team.

1938 WORLD AMATEUR BASEBALL CHAMPIONSHIP

Venue	Score
Liverpool	3 – 0
Hull	8 – 6
Rochdale	0 – 5
Halifax	4 – 0
Leeds	5 - 3

Lancashire Beaten

AMERICANS TOO GOOD AT BASEBALL

"Stars" Who Failed to Find Form

LANCASHIRE'S baseball team, chosen from the county's crack sides in the Lancashire-Yorkshire Major League, gave an insipid display against America at Watersheddings on Saturday night and in the presence of a crowd of over two thousand was well and truly whacked by the side representing America.

Lancashire's work on the diamond lacked all snap and fire, and individuals who are stars with their own clubs seemed to have no life about them when playing with the county side.

Perhaps it was because they were playing before their own supporters on their own diamond that prompted the Oldham members of the team to snap out a bit, and it is a fact that Ross Kendrick and Jack Culverwell, of the Greyhounds outfit, saved Lancashire from utter rout.

LANCASHIRE	7
AMERICA	11

BASEALL

Bolton Scarlets Well Beaten

GREYHOUNDS NOT TROUBLED

Pitcher, Alan Forrest aged 18 was the youngest club professional in the Lancashire and Yorkshire Major Baseball League.

Rees And Forrest The Stars

THE first ball game of the season at Watersheddings failed to produce any real thrills, for Bolton Scarlets were well beaten by Oldham Greyhounds to the tune of nine runs to two, and the result was never in any real doubt after the first frame. Pitcher Forrest was hit only five times during the match, though if the Bolton batsmen had looked them over a little better they might have done a considerable amount of walking. The highlights of the match were a homer from Craven, of Bolton, and two spectacular outfield catches from Tommy Rees, the Oldham Rugby full-back.

Tommy Rees- a crack outfielder was considered the best "home grown" player in the North West. He represented both Lancashire and England at Baseball.

TOMMY REES AND BEN CRONSHAW

Ken Lowe takes a tackle watched by Fred Hall and Norman Pugh. Action from the game against Rochdale on Easter Monday 1938.
Result: Oldham 22 Rochdale H. 7.

Billy Moore and Edgar Brookes advance on the Huddersfield left winger, Ray Markham, in the match at Watersheddings on February 5th 1938.
Result: Oldham 13 Huddersfield 8.

HIGGINSHAW RUGBY FOOTBALL CLUB.

Hon Secretary: F. S. Wallwork, 15, Caley St, Higginshaw, Oldham.
Headquarters HARE & HOUNDS, Higginshaw.

Dear Sir,   Date as Postmark
                                                 Friday
You have been selected to play on Saturday next,

against *Paris Students*   at *Watersheddings*

Meet at *Headquarters 9.30*, Kick-off *11.0* AM.

If unable to play, REPLY AT ONCE, and oblige,
Yours faithfully,

F. S. Wallwork

A team group from a match between Higginshaw and Paris University played at Watersheddings on Good Friday 1938.
Inset: A selection card for one of the Higginshaw players.

OLDHAM FOOTBALL CLUB

WATERSHEDDINGS, OLDHAM.

Saturday, 30th April, 1938

KICK-OFF 3-30 P.M.

FRED W. ASHWORTH'S BENEFIT

Produced by the courtesy of the "Oldham Chronicle."

J. Allan Hanson & Son Ltd., Printers, Cross St., Oldham.

Referee: Mr. W. WOOD

Touch Judges: Mr W. WOOLAM and Mr. W. BURKE

OLDHAM
Red and White Jerseys.

1. Rees, T. E.
2. Hall, F.
3. Davies, C.
4. Rhydderch, V.
5. Hague, I.
6. Barnes, H.
7. Smith, A. R.
8. Read, J.
9. Cunliffe, S.
10. Rees, L.
11. Moore, W. J.
12. Elson, F.
13. Pugh, N. (Capt.)

Hearne, J.
Bates, E. E.

Mr. G. F. Hutchin's Team
White Jerseys.

1 Goldie, G. W.,
   Leeds and Featherstone
2 Rix, S.,
   Oldham and Broughton
3 Madden, D.,
   Huddersfield
4 Francis, L. B.,
   Wigan
5 Jenkins, T.,
   Swinton
6 Jenkins, E.,
   Salford and Wigan
7 McCue, T.,
   Widnes
8 Silcock, N.,
   Widnes
9 Thomas, W. T.,
   Wigan
10 Stoddart, J.,
   Swinton
11 Cattlin, R.,
   Huddersfield
12 Arkwright, J.,
   Warrington
13 Butters, F.,
   Swinton

Taylor, F.,
   Huddersfield

Fred Ashworth leads out the Oldham team captained by Norman Pugh for his benefit game on April 30th 1938. The opposition under the guidance of Oldham official George Hutchins included some of the game's stars, and Sid Rix was persuaded to put in an appearance. Sad note is that both of the Oldham reserves, Jack Hearne and Ted Bates, were killed in the Second World War.

GREENACRES 20

Colours : RED AND WHITE JERSEYS.

1—F.B. :
W. YATES

2—R.W. :   3—C. :   4—L.W. :

A. BELL   G. BOWDEN   D. GOUGH

5—O.H. :   6—S.H. :

H. CLARK (capt)   F. BIRD

7—F. :   8—F. :

N. TAYLOR   D. ROBINSON

9—F. :   10—F. :   11—F. :

J. BIRCHALL   G. PICKFORD   T. DOCKERTY

| DO NOT FORGET TO HAND IN YOUR BALLOT CARD |

F. TAYLOR   J. EDWARDS   W. WORRALL

11—F. :   10—F. :   9—F. :

E. WILLIAMSON   F. FARRELL

8—F. :   7—F. :

L. GALLOWAY   A. WHITAKER

6—S.H. :   5—O.H. :

A. GRINDROD   H. SUNDERLAND   J. FOY

4—L.W. :   3—C. :   2—R.W. :

W. BINNS
1—F.B. :

FERRANTI 8

Colours : BLUE AND WHITE JERSEYS.

Experimental 11-a-side Rugby League game at Watersheddings, Oldham.

FERRANTI

(for HIGGINSHAW) *v.*

GREENACRES

Saturday, May 14th. 1938,

. . . *Kick-off 3-0 p.m.* . . .

Referee : Mr. W. WOOD.

Touch Judges :
Messrs. W. WOOLAM and S. COLLINS.

Timekeeper : Mr. G. F. HUTCHINS.

Official Programme   -   Price 1d.

Programme for an experimental 11-a-side match between Ferranti and Greenacres at Watersheddings on May 14th 1938.

In addition to the 11-a-side experiment an official timekeeper was used to relieve the referee of that anxiety!

At least this latter innovation actually came to be when it was introduced in 1972.

A. BELL.

PICKFORD

T. DOCKERTY.

J. EDWARDS.

In addition to the 11-a-side game, other experiments will consist of an Official Timekeeper to relieve the referee of that anxiety ; an earlier kick-off time than 3-30 ; minimum distance for the scrums from touchline to be 10 yards and the referee to stand on the narrow side to enable him to observe the offside tactics, etc., resorted to; and finally the taking of the Law relating to "a scrum" on page 32 of the Official Guide literally, the defending Half-back placing the ball on the ground between forwards in readiness, and then retiring behind his side of the pack. Verbal commands from the Referee of "FORM" and "GO" will be readily understood when seen in practice. The scrummage solution at last !

Caricatures of some of the players in the 11-a-side experimental game and a summary of what the experiment was all about.

Maypole Dance At Scholars' Sports

Chronicle photograph.

Rain curtailed the programme for the Oldham schoolchildrens' annual sports day at the Watersheddings Football ground, on Tuesday. The organisers did manage however to include in the completed events the infants' contribution—a series of Maypole dances. Weather permitting the programme will be completed on the ground on Monday evening, starting at 6 45.

Lancashire-Yorkshire Major League

BASEBALL

AT

WATERSHEDDINGS

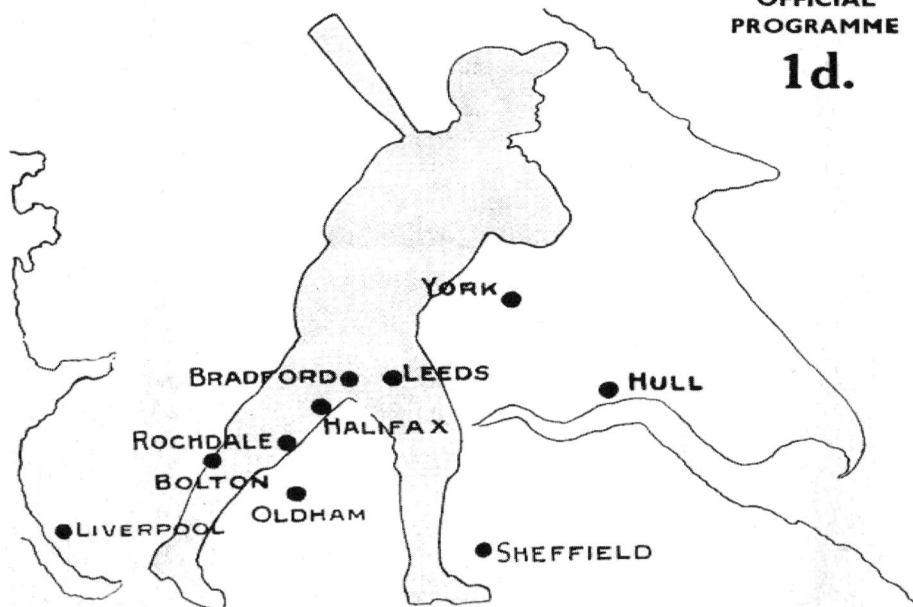

YORK

BRADFORD · LEEDS · HULL

ROCHDALE · HALIFAX

BOLTON

LIVERPOOL · OLDHAM

· SHEFFIELD

OLDHAM Greyhounds v LEEDS, Wednesday, August 24th, 6-45 p.m.

BATTING ORDER.

No.	Oldham Greyhounds		No.	Leeds	
3	J. DAVY	1st Base	10	W. SHARP	Catcher
9	F. FAULKNER	Left Field	2	D. DESAULNIER	Pitcher
4	K. ROBINSON	2nd Base	4	H. HOLMES	Right Field
2	R. KENDRICK	Pitcher	7	T. McNEIL	Short Stop
1	J. CULVERWELL	Catcher	9	B. CRUISE	1st Base
5	A. FORREST	Short Stop	3	M. CHOULER	Left Field
7	T. REES	Right Field	11	D. TANNARD	3rd Base
6	E. RUSHBY	3rd Base	8	M. TAYLOR	2nd Base
8	H. CRONSHAW	Centre Field	6	D. BATESON	Centre Field

Benchers—10 DYMENT
          11 THORPE
          12 STEVENS

Benchers—12 Bob OLIVER
          5 Jack ARCHER

INNINGS	1	2	3	4	5	6	7	8	9	TOTAL
GREYHOUNDS	0	4	0	1	0	2				7
LEEDS	0	0	0	0	3	0				3

Chief Umpire : WHITEHEAD   Base Umpire : TONGE
Commentator : E. L. TURNER

Field and Player Positions

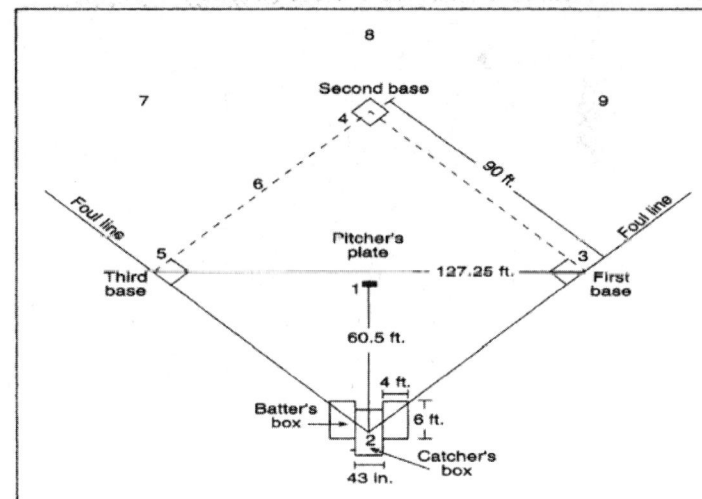

Second base

90 ft.

Foul line   Foul line

Pitcher's plate

Third base   127.25 ft.   First base

60.5 ft.

4 ft.

Batter's box   6 ft.   Catcher's box

43 in.

1 Pitcher
2 Catcher
3 First baseman
4 Second baseman
5 Third baseman
6 Shortstop
7 Left fielder
8 Center fielder
9 Right fielder

1939

FERRANTI - Winners of the Standard Cup in 1937 & 1938 and runners-up in 1939.
Back Row: S. Cattlin, F. Taylor, W. Wood, F. Farrell, J. Brierley, W. Barnes, E. Williamson, J. Edwards.
Front Row: T. Nield, T. Dalton, L. Bayliffe, A. Grindrod, A. Whittaker, W. Binns, J. Hardman, J. Lees.

1939

Pre-season trial match played in August 1939. "Blues" v "Reds"
Back Row: *A. Givvons, E. Brooks, M. Maloney, N. Pugh, W. Moore, F. Parr, H. Tufnell (trainer).*
Front Row: *D. Schofield, G. Thomas, W. Stott, E. Kerwick, E. Large, J. Turner, V. Rhydderch.*

1939

Back Row: F. Elson, K. Lowe, S. Cunliffe, F. Marsh, J. Greenwood, M. Downey.
Front Row: A. Garnett, W. Mitchell, J. Read, F. Hall, R. Smith, V. Kenny, Mr. W. Wood (ref.).

1939
-40
50
YEARS
AND
STILL
GOING
STRONG.
OLDHAM RUGBY LEAGUE CLUB

ADOLF IS TO BLAME

WHAT MIGHT HAVE BEEN!

WHAT MIGHT HAVE BEEN!

An amusing cartoon from the Green Final in 1940 alluding to the fact that Oldham players Edgar Brooks and Alec Givvons were being tipped for selection for the 1940 tour to Australia and New Zealand.

The original caption read as follows:
"But for the outbreak of war, two Oldham players, Edgar Brooks and Alex Givvons, would have been well in the running for places in the R.L. team which should have toured Australia this summer. The tour has, of course, been cancelled."

OLDHAM FOOTBALL CLUB

PROGRAMME
OFFICIAL

ENGLAND

WALES

AT WATERSHEDDINGS
OLDHAM,
NOVEMBER 9th, 1940

PRICE 2d.

Programme for the wartime international played at Watersheddings on November 9th 1940. England defeated Wales by eight points to five aided by local born Edgar Brooks at hooker.

NORTHERN RUGBY LEAGUE

International Match

ENGLAND v. WALES

At Watersheddings, OLDHAM

Saturday, November 9th, 1940.

TEAMS

ENGLAND	WALES
1. BELSHAW (Warrington) (Capt.)	1. JONES (Wigan)
2. BATTEN (Hunslet)	2. WALTERS (Bradford)
3. WARING (St. Helens)	3. RISMAN (Salford) (Capt.)
4. LAWRENSON (Wigan)	4. EVANS (Leeds)
5. PEAKE (Warrington)	5. WILLIAMS (Salford)
6. TRACEY (St. Helens)	6. MORRIS (Leeds)
7. McCUE (Widnes)	7. JENKINS (Leeds)
8. ROBERTS (Widnes)	8. WHITCOMBE (Bradford)
9. BROOKS (Oldham)	9. MURPHY (Leeds)
10. IRVING (Halifax)	10. HUGHES (Swinton)
11. TATTERSFIELD (Leeds)	11. THOMAS (W.T.) (Wigan)
12. BUNTER (Broughton)	12. ORFORD (Wakefield)
13. MOORE (Bradford)	13. FOSTER (Bradford)
BROGDEN (Hull)	LEWIS (Swinton)
FLOWERS (Wakefield)	

England—White jerseys.   Wales—Red jerseys.

Referee: Mr. G. F. PHILLIPS (Widnes)

DEWSBURY RUGBY LEAGUE FOOTBALL CLUB

Rugby League Cup Winners 1912 — Runners Up 1929,
Yorkshire Cup Winners — 1925 & 1927.

EDWARD M. WARING
SECRETARY-MANAGER

Resident
Tel.   EAST VIEW,
1471.   HOLLINROYD ROAD
            DEWSBURY

TEL. 531.

Crown Flatt
Dewsbury

April 1941

Dear Sir,

If you can get over to Watersheddings on Saty Apl 12th I should like to see you. I may be able to fine you a game.

Kind Regards
Yours faithfully,

Edw Waring

A letter from the famous Eddie Waring to Albert Bell. The future BBC commentator, then manager of Dewsbury, was requesting Bell to attend Watersheddings for the match on April 12th 1941.

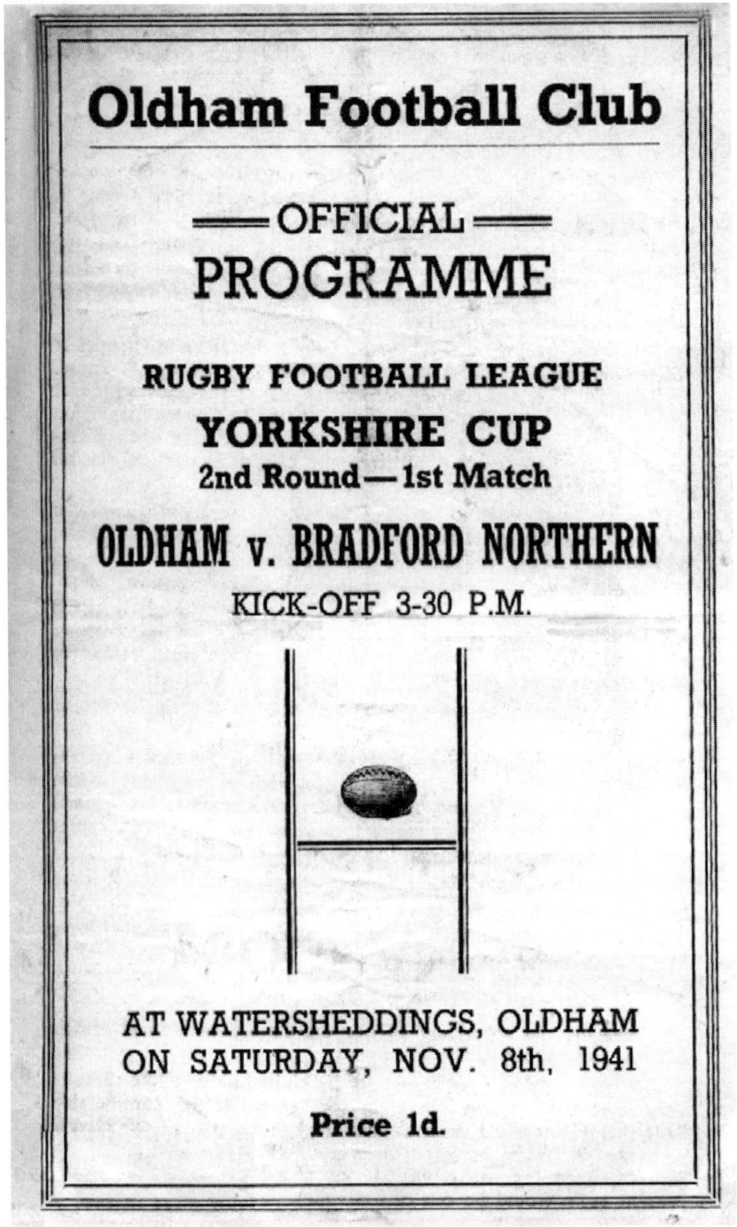

Oldham Football Club

— OFFICIAL —

PROGRAMME

RUGBY FOOTBALL LEAGUE

YORKSHIRE CUP

2nd Round — 1st Match

OLDHAM v. BRADFORD NORTHERN

KICK-OFF 3-30 P.M.

AT WATERSHEDDINGS, OLDHAM
ON SATURDAY, NOV. 8th, 1941

Price 1d.

Strange but true!
An Oldham programme featuring the Roughyeds in the Yorkshire Cup!

Due to the shortage of teams continuing to play during the war, certain of the Lancashire clubs were invited to play in the "white rose" competition.

Although Oldham won the second leg 9 - 5, Bradford's 10 - 0 victory in this game was enough to see them through. The Oldham captain (pictured above) was Billy Stott, who became the first winner of the Lance Todd trophy when playing for Wakefield in the 1946 Challenge Cup final.

RUGBY FOOTBALL LEAGUE

YORKSHIRE CUP—2nd Round (1st Match).

Oldham v. Bradford Northern

AT WATERSHEDDINGS,

SATURDAY, NOVEMBER 8th, 1941. KICK-OFF 3-30 p.m.

OLDHAM (Red and White Jerseys)	BRADFORD NORTHERN (Red, Amber and Black Jerseys)
1. THOMAS	1. CARMICHAEL
2. WILLIAMS	2. BEST
3. DAGNAN	3. BILLINGTON
4. MITCHELL	4. WARD, E.
5. TAYLOR, F.	5. WALTERS
6. STOTT (Capt.)	6. KAY
7. BOWYER	7. WARD, D.
8. WHITEHEAD	8. WHITCOMBE
9. BROOKS	9. CARTER
10. GREENWOOD	10. HIGSON
11. LOWE	11. FOSTER
12. AMBLER	12. SMITH
13. CATTLIN	13. HUTCHINSON
— OGDEN, H.	— MURRAY
	— BENNETT.

Referee : Mr. E. DEVINE (Leeds).

Touch Judges : Mr. A. BURGE and Mr. C. A. MOSELY.

A little good news for our supporters and the Rugby League generally is that Alex Givvons has now commenced training, and that points to one thing that Alex is going to play football again, and for his own club.

It is a long time since he had a game and naturally a little time must elapse before he appears back in the team, as Alex himself feels that he must be thoroughly fit before he can do himself justice and justice to the game.

During the war time period many clubs used "guest" players and Oldham were no exception. Pictured here are some of the game's finest who became temporary "Roughyeds".
Above: Ken Gee and Joe Egan (Wigan)
Above (right): Willy Horne (Barrow)
Left: Gus Risman (Salford)
Right: Tommy McCue and Tommy Shannon (Widnes)

1945

OLDHAM F.C. 1945-46.

Standing: C. Sutcliffe, W. Wood, T. Rostron, H. Ogden, W. Frost, T. Ayres, H.D. Shaw, S. Inglesfield, J. Heywood, G.F. Hutchins.
Seated: F. Lees, D. Rees, N. Harris, N. Pugh, G. Gummer, W. Griffiths, V. Kenny.

A trio of Roughyed Welsh Internationals.

Norman Pugh
Back-row forward
363 appearances
1933-48.

Doug Phillips
Second-row forward
Toured with the 1946 British Lions and played in
all three tests against Australia.

Norman Harris
Centre three-quarter
119 appearances
1945-49.

1946

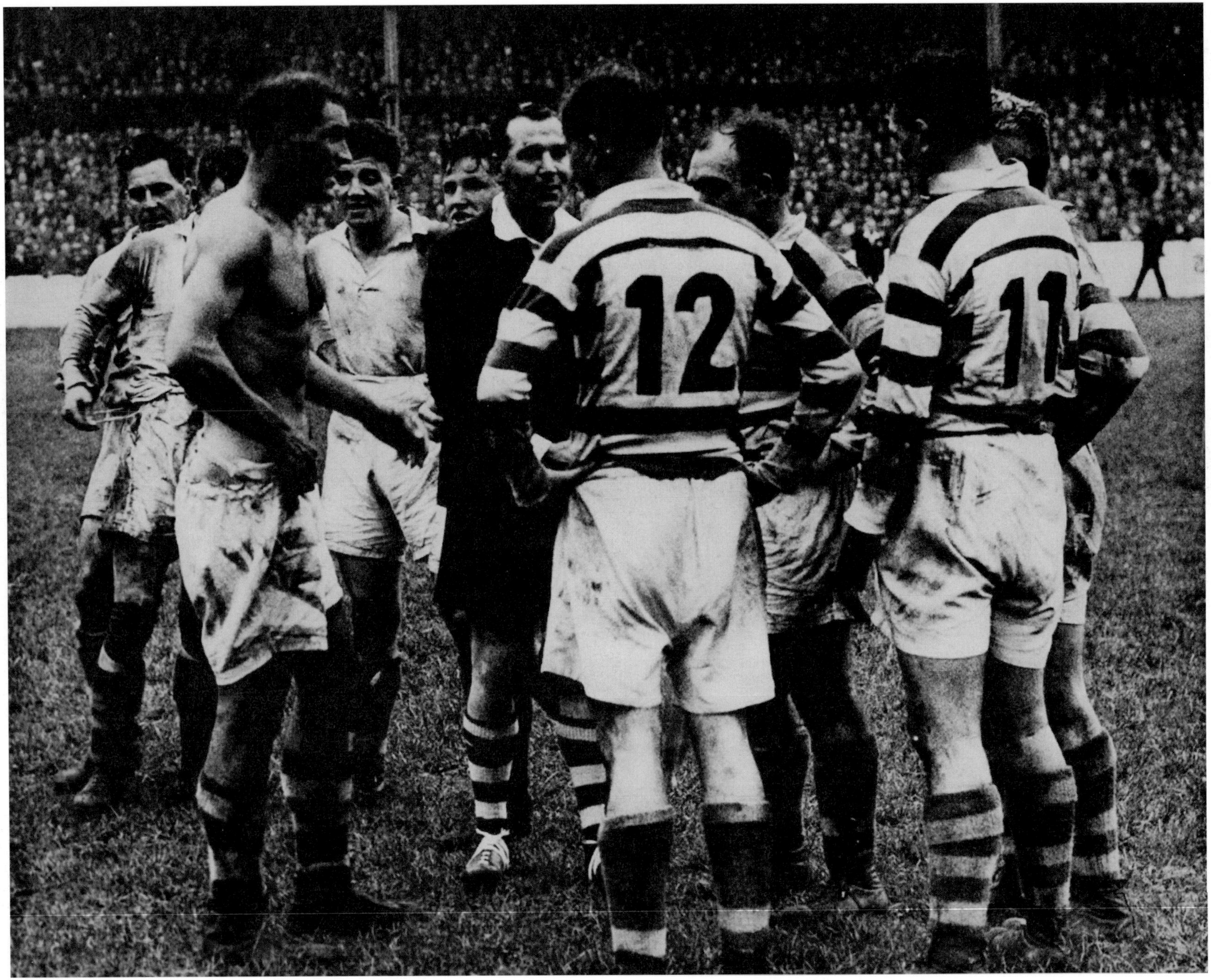

Stand off between the Oldham and Wigan forwards with
Oldham's international second-row forward Doug Phillips
(shirtless) in the midst of the confrontation in the image opposite.

Above: Wigan legend Ken Gee helps complete a tackle on an
Oldham player (in the white strip) as Harry Ogden and Doug
Shaw look on.

Right: Norman Harris clears the Oldham line under pressure
from Eddie Watkins as Dai Rees and Norman Pugh watch with
interest.

Over 16,000 spectators turned up for this Lancashire Cup semi-
final played on October 15th 1946.

Result: Oldham 7 Wigan 21.

Crossley the Castleford prop-forward is well tackled in the match at Watersheddings on November 16th 1946, with Edgar Brooks, Billy Moore and Doug Shaw ready to finish the job. Result: Oldham 8 Castleford 5.

Tommy Ayres makes a tackle against Rochdale on New Years Day 1947. Other Oldham players left to right, Harry Ogden, Ray Smith and Les Thomas. Result: Oldham 32 Rochdale 5.

German prisoners of war, interned at the Glen Mill site, remove snow from the Watersheddings' pitch during the harsh winter in January 1947.

More deep snow at 'sheddings in February 1947.

The only match to beat the 1947 freeze at Watersheddings between January 18th and March 25th was the cup tie against Belle Vue Rangers on February 22nd. Here we see Harry Ogden and Edgar Brooks close in on the Rangers player Powell.
Note the poor state of the main stand roof and the condemned top tier of the Waterhead end "Penny Rush".

Local engineering worker Billy Wood was featured in an Oldham Chronicle series of "players at work".

A back row forward, Billy played 68 first team matches for Oldham between 1943 and 1948.

Les Thomas takes on the Halifax defence with Harry Ogden in support.
Action from the match at Watersheddings on September 27th 1947.
Result: Oldham 13 Halifax 0.

Norman Pugh Benefit

On April 22nd 1947 Oldham played "Jim Sullivan's team" in a benefit match for veteran Welsh forward Norman Pugh.
Shown above is a promotional poster and a photograph of Alex Givvons and Norman (the two captains) shaking hands before the kick off.
For the record, Oldham lost 16 - 24 but Norman was amongst the try scorers for the Roughyeds.

1947

Higginshaw: Victors over Ferranti by 16 – 4 in the 1947 Standard Cup final.
Back Row *(Players): Robinson, Jennings, Carroll, Maloney, Taylor, Webb, Houghton.*
Front Row: *Heap. Thomas. Howarth, Meredith, Hindley, Dyson.*

"Higgy" captain, Ron Meredith, receives the trophy from the Mayor, councillor J. Berry.
A talented stand-off half, Ron played for Oldham during the Second World War period.

Alex Givvons brings down a Wakefield player in the match on January 20th 1948. Other Oldham players left to right: Norman Pugh, Norman Thompson, Harry Ogden and Joe Mahoney. Result: Oldham 5 Wakefield T. 24.

The Oldham line-up also included guest players.
Back Row: J. Heywood, N. Pugh, W. Wood,
L. Thomas, H. Ogden, J. Taylor, S. Inglesfield,
P. Devery, W. Mitchell.
Front Row: J. Mundy, N. Harris, J. Mahoney,
A.R. Smith, S. McCormick, R. Pepperell.

Back Row: F. Ashworth (Oldham coach), P. Reid
(Huddersfield), C. Smith (Halifax), C. Brereton (Leeds),
J. McDonald (Halifax),
B. Bevan (Warrington), J. Hunter (Huddersfield),
E. McDonald (Halifax), L. Cooper (Huddersfield),
A. Givvons (Oldham).
Front Row: A. Clues (Leeds), E. Brooks (Oldham), H. Bath
(Warrington), H. Cook (Leeds) , K. Rika (Halifax).

On April 27th 1948 Oldham played an Empire XIII in a benefit match for long serving hooker, Edgar Brooks.

The star studded Empire line-up, which included Edgar, triumphed 33 - 24 in front of 7,000 spectators.

July 24th 1948 saw a sports review at Watersheddings in co-ordination with the Central Council of Recreation (Manchester).
The programme included: Wrestling, Boxing, Bicycle Polo, Gymnastics, Athletics, Heading Tennis and Scottish Country Dancing.

No doubt one of the big attractions at the sports gala must have been a special four-a-side football exhibition which brought the two teams of star players pictured here:

Dark shirts left to right: Johnny Morris, Jack Rowley and Stan Pearson of Manchester United and Frank Swift of Manchester City.
White shirts left to right: Stan Mortensen of Blackpool with Willie McIntosh, Bill Shankly and Tom Finney of Preston North End.

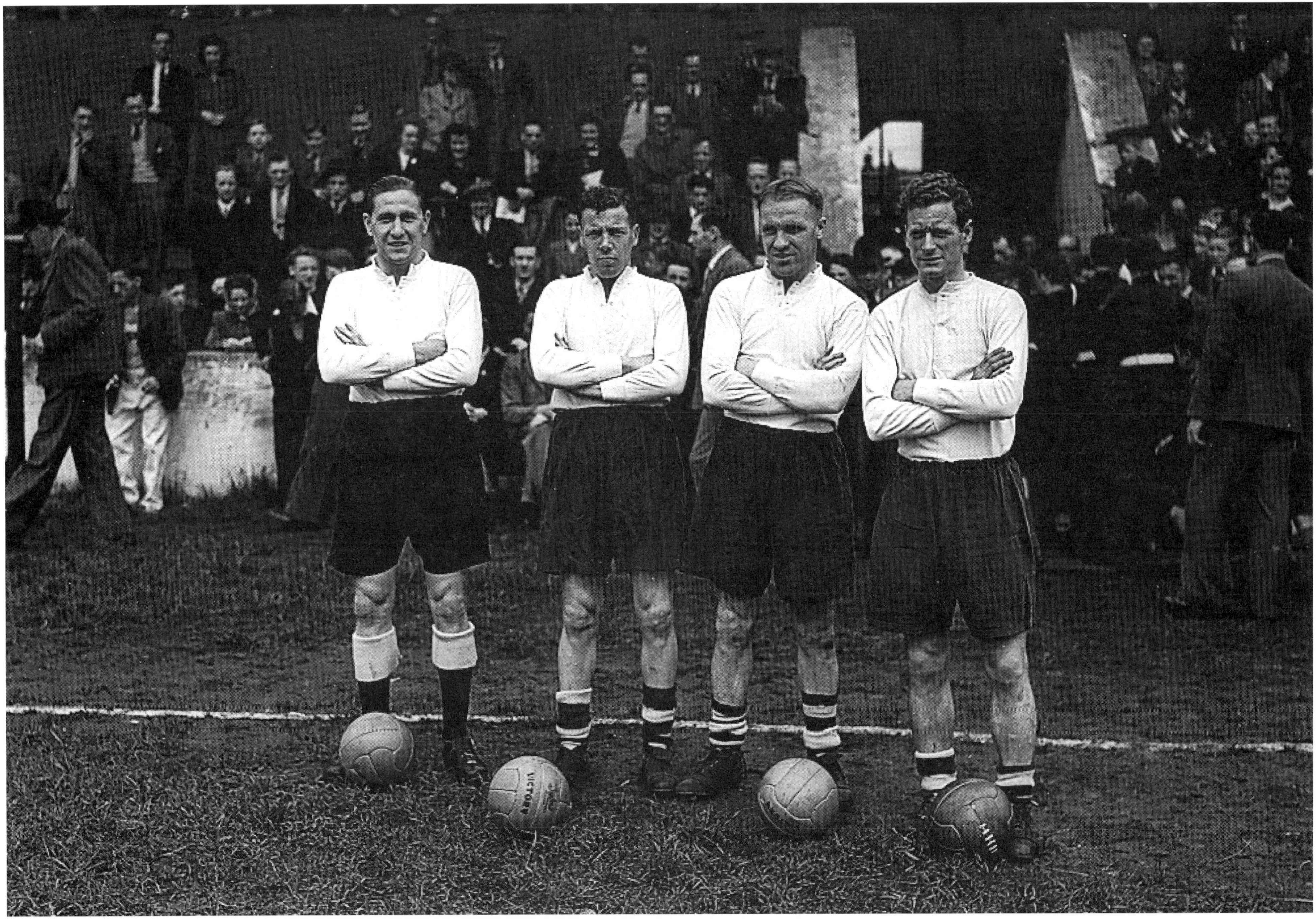
VICTORY

August 1948 and the Oldham players are seen in training for the new season.
Left to right:
Stan Inglesfield, Bert Ambler, Glan Jones, Harry Ogden, Billy Mitchell, Les Thomas,
Edgar Brooks, Norman Harris, Jack Taylor.

September 14th 1948 and the "Gartside" plan is tested in a specially arranged match between Higginshaw and the "Rest" of the Oldham amateur league. In the hope of creating more attractive play, the three-quarters had to leave a 20 yard gap between teams at the scrum, as can be seen in the photograph.
History would teach us that the idea didn't catch on.

Oldham and Wakefield schoolboys play in a curtain raiser to the senior match on October 9th 1948.

G.F. HUTCHINS
Memorial Fund

1949

OLDHAM F.C.
Supporters Club

All Proceeds to be Devoted to the Above

1/-

In 1949 an appeal was launched to raise funds to reconstruct the "Penny Rush" stand at the Waterhead Park end of the ground, thereafter to be named the Hutchins stand after the long serving Oldham official, George F. Hutchins.

A momento of the appeal was the brochure shown here and contained within its pages, an advert for the greyhound stadium.

YOU'D BE SURPRISED.

How Pleasantly the time Passes if you :—

Go Greyhound Racing at your local track !

OLDHAM STADIUM

RACING

TUESDAYS & THURSDAYS
AT 7-15 P.M.

ELECTRIC TOTALISATOR
FORECAST, AND WIN AND PLACE

ADMISSION 2/9   LADIES 1/9

OLDHAM
FOOTBALL CLUB

OLDHAM
v.
BROUGHTON MOOR

1st Round R L. Challenge Cup. (1st Leg)

at Watersheddings

Saturday, 12th February, 1949

Kick-off 3-0 p.m.

Official Programme - 2d.

Gordon Whittaker Ltd., Printers, Oldham.

BROUGHTON MOOR R.L.F.C.

RUGBY LEAGUE CUP (1st Round—2nd Leg).

BROUGHTON MOOR
VERSUS
OLDHAM

BOROUGH PARK GROUND

SATURDAY, FEBRUARY 19th, 1949

Kick-off 3-0 p.m.

In February 1949 Oldham played Cumbrian amateurs Broughton Moor in a two-leg Challenge Cup first round tie. The first leg at Watersheddings ended with a convincing Oldham victory 30 - 0 and the following week the Cumbrians fared no better going down 35 - 2 at Workington's Borough Park ground. Here we see Oldham captain Edgar Brooks before the kick-off at Watersheddings with the Broughton Moor skipper, Stephen Nicholson, under the watchful eye of referee, Mr. F. Cottam of Wakefield.

The Oldham team that defeated Broughton Moor at Watersheddings on February 12th 1949.
Back Row: Harry Ogden, Arthur Tomlinson, John Sugden, Irving Barraclough, Harold Tomlinson, Frank Daley, Jack Casey.
Front Row: Wilson Spencer, Tommy Leyland, Edgar Brooks, Glan Jones, Billy Mitchell, Ken Ward.

Oldham stand-off, Ken Ward, moves in to complete the tackle on Halifax winger Kia Rika as Glan Jones and Frank Daley look on. This third round cup tie attracted the biggest crowd of the 1940s to Watersheddings but Halifax emerged victorious by seven points to two. Over 20,000 people witnessed a tremendous defensive effort from the Yorkshiremen who went on to reach the final at Wembley where they lost to Bradford Northern. All this after finishing 25th out of 30 teams in the league!

*Oldham prop-forwards Harold Tomlinson and Harry Ogden wait for the
play-the-ball in the match against Barrow on January 22nd 1949.
Result: Oldham 5 Barrow 8.*

Whoosh - Strike Three!
Reese, the Manchester pitcher and number one bat, strikes out as the ball lands safely in the Burtonwood catcher's glove.

OLDHAM GREYHOUND STADIUM.
WATERSHEDDINGS.

Saturday, May 7th 1949

AMERICAN
AIR FORCE
V
Manchester and
District League.

IF YOU HAVE NOTHING TO DO TO-NIGHT
DANCE
WITH THESE BOYS
AT CHADDERTON TOWN HALL.
GRAND BAND   LICENSED BAR.   ADMISSION 3 -

Programme - - Threepence.

Programmes are being sold by Chadderton Grammar School Rover Crew
in aid of Bob-a-Job Fund.

Manchester District.		Burtonwood Eagles.	
1—REESE	Pitcher.	1—SHAFER	Pitcher.
2—GARDNER	Catcher.	2—HOFFER	Catcher.
3—LOMAS	1st Base.	3—HUNT	1st Base.
4—KERSHAW	2nd Base.	4—HURSKEY	2nd Base.
5—LEANORD	3rd Base.	5—TARNEROW	3rd Base.
6—HUDDLESTONE	Short Stop.	6—NIEL	Short Stop.
7—LEACH	Left Field.	7—PEPPER	Left Field.
8—TAYLOR	Centre Field.	8—SLAYTON	Centre Field.
9—BRIERLEY	Right Field.	9—GALUIN	Right Field.

Benchers / Benchers

10—Yearsley / 10—Allan
11—Silk / 11—Mather
12—Waterhouse / 12—Wheeler
13—Mullins / 13—Rubins
14—Tyldsley / 14—Norton
15—Nelson / 15—Jordan
16—Sainsbury

Umpire :- ELLIS.
Umpire :- Lieutenant ANDERSON.

Baseball returned to Watersheddings in May 1949.

The photograph shows a team that represented the Manchester and District League including two Oldham players and their opponents from the U.S. army air force base at Burtonwood.

New turf had been laid and is inspected by groundsman Shaw and committee men Coulthard and Hartley.

First match on the new turf was the pre-season trial match. In the photo winger Bob Batten up-ends loose-forward Tommy Leyland.

Prior to the start of the 1949-50 season new showers had been installed at Watersheddings and in the photo on the left Tommy Rostron can be seen trying them out after the trial match on August 6th 1949.

Ken Traill prepares to kick at a packed Watersheddings for the Challenge Cup first round, first leg match played before a crowd of over 18,000 spectators on February 4th 1950.
Result: Oldham 5 Bradford N. 16.

1950

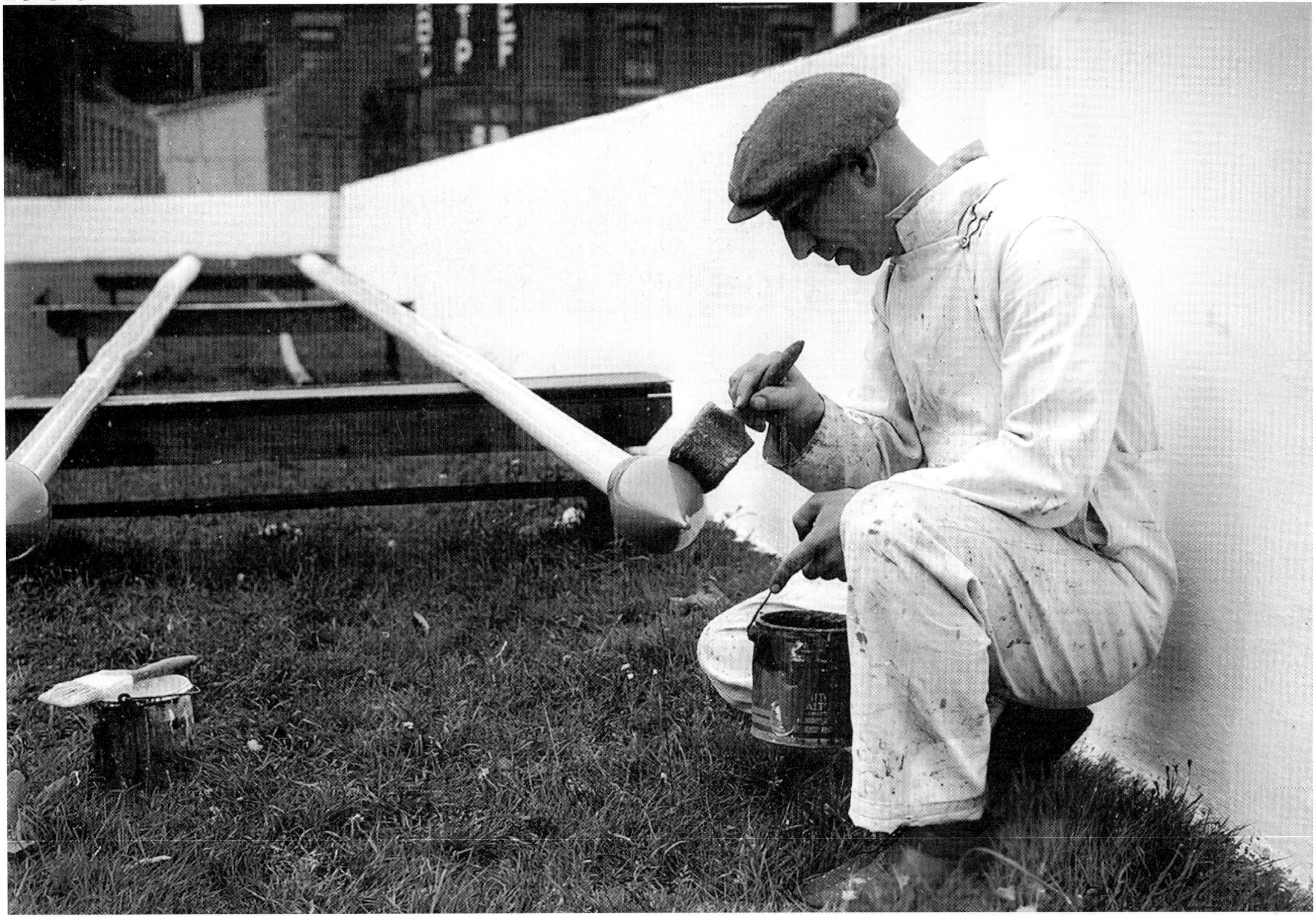

New goal posts are erected on August 12th 1950.

Here they can be seen being painted by Oldham hooker and painter and decorator by trade, Edgar Brooks, before being planted into the ground.

Oldham "hard-man" Arthur Tomlinson makes a burst through the Wakefield defence in the match at Watersheddings on September 9th 1950. Other Oldham players from left to right: Les Anthony, Tommy Leyland and Jack Taylor.
Result: Oldham 35 Wakefield T. 8.

Bryn Day, Charlie Winslade and Jack Keith gather around one of their colleagues who has brought down Cox the Liverpool full-back on March 3rd 1951.
Result: Oldham 16 Liverpool 3.

1951

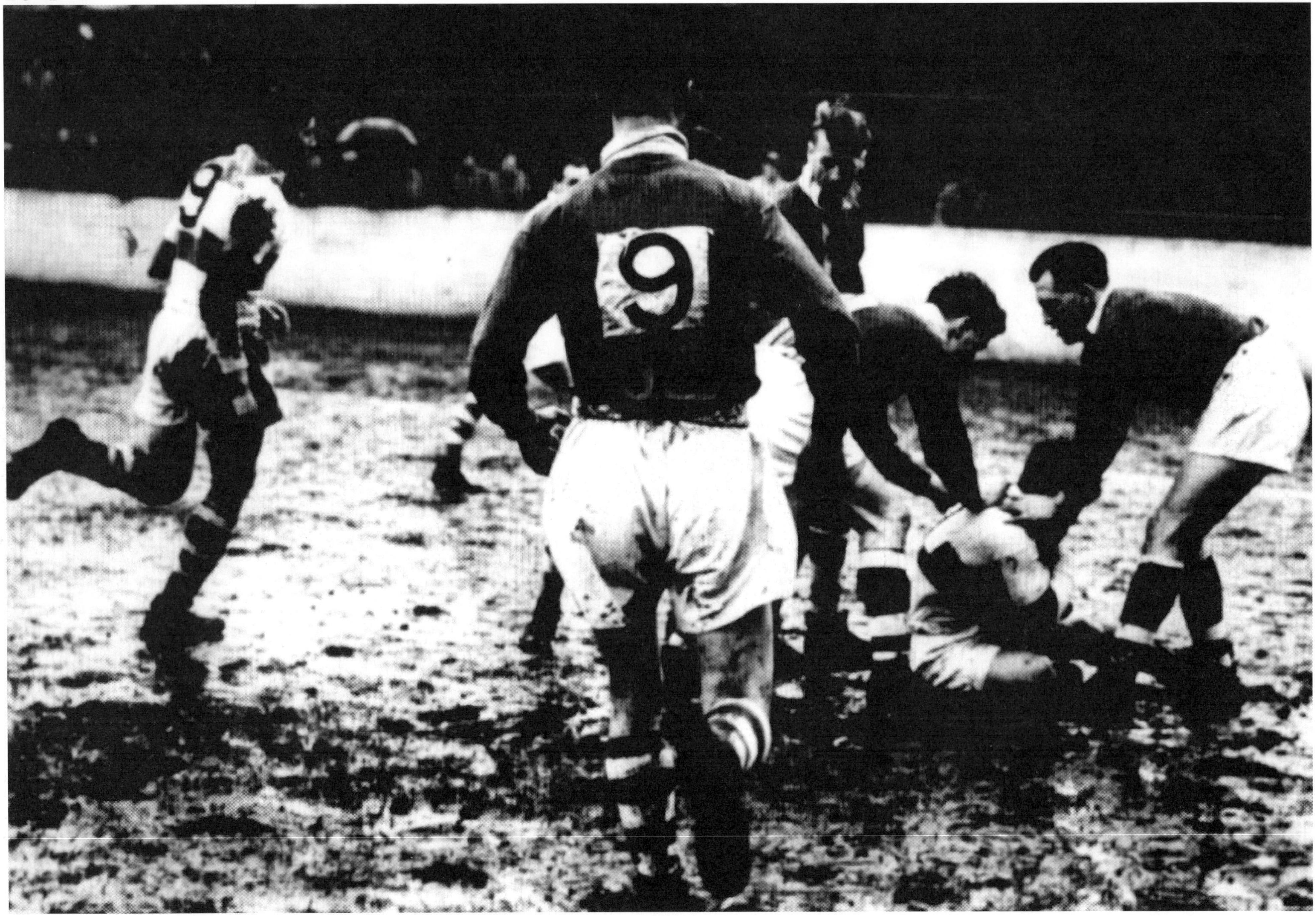

As the Oldham Tinkers famously once sang: "At Watersheddings it used be good to see 'em fight for't ball in't mud."
They could have been singing about the match against St Helens on March 26th 1951 when the game had to be abandoned at
half-time with Oldham leading by three points to nil, because the players and officials couldn't tell the teams apart.
The image opposite was taken early in the match, whereas the one below shows the deterioration of the pitch
and the jerseys now caked in mud leaving the players unrecognisable.

1951

The Oldham team that beat Leigh 15 - 11 on October 20th 1951. An unusual line-up in so much as ace wingman Joe Warham played at stand-off.
Back Row: *Ken Jackson, Harry Ogden, Les Anthony, Arthur Tomlinson, Charlie Winslade, Bernard Ganley.*
Middle Row: *Terry O' Grady, Billy Mitchell, Bryn Goldswain, Lawrie Platt, Alan Davies.*　　**Front Row**: *Joe Warham, Frank Stirrup.*

The opening match of the 1951-52 season played on August 18th saw Oldham off to a winning start. In the photo we can see Harry Ogden advancing on a Bradford player with Bryn Day keeping watch in the background

The first try of the match went to Joe Warham (right) who would fininsh the season as the club's leading try scorer for the third consecutive year.

Result: Oldham 11 Bradford N. 7.

1952

Oldham centre Billy Mitchell takes on the Featherstone defence on the opening day of the 1952-53 season on August 23rd. Notice the top tier of the "Penny Rush" stand still lies empty awaiting renovation. Result: Oldham 32 Featherstone 8.

Oldham winger Lionel Emmitt is tackled by Jimmy Honey and Peter Metcalfe of St Helens on April 18th 1953 while Alan Davies and George Langfield keep a close watch. Result: Oldham 13 St Helens 14.

Oldham Schools Sports Association form a human E II R as part of the ongoing Coronation celebrations for Queen Elizabeth II, in July 1953.
Notice the absence of the Hutchins Stand, now completely demolished. It was rebuilt for the following rugby season.

Schoolboys make up human pyramids as part of the Coronation celebration.

Possibly the best ball-playing exponent the club ever had on the books!
A classic image of Frank Stirrup preparing to send an inside pass to Terry O'Grady with Billy Mitchell in the background.
Action from the match against Wigan on August 15th 1953.
Result: Oldham 18 Wigan 7.

March 6th 1954 Terry O'Grady halts the progress of Brian Bevan in the second round of the Challenge Cup at Watersheddings. Sid Little is seen moving in to finish the job!
However, Bev had the last laugh scoring the only try in a seven points to four victory for the "Wire".

TOUR REPRESENTATIVE

Terry O'Grady
Oldham born winger who toured Australia and New Zealand in 1954 playing in five out of the six tests.

In the bleak mid-winter
January, 1955

OUTSIDE:
*The buses line up on the approaches
to a snow-covered Watersheddings.*

INSIDE:
*The players of Oldham and Warrington slug it out in
the snow.
Result: Oldham 8 Warrington 12.*

If you are going to win a cup-tie you might as well do it in style. Alan Davies dives over for the only try in the five points to two victory over Wigan in the first round of the Challenge Cup on February 21st 1955. Over 22,000 spectators were in attendance. Oldham players left to right: Harry Ogden, Ken Jackson, Alan Davies, Sid Little and Terry O'Grady.

Frank Pitchford is congratulated by his team mates after one of his two tries in the game against Leigh on April 16th 1955.
The scores ended level at 15 points each. Note the now renamed "Hutchins Stand", though reduced in size, is now back in use.
Oldham players left to right: Charlie Winslade, Ken Jackson, Jack Keith, Frank Pitchford, John Etty and Dick Cracknell.

A police escort is required for the Hull captain Roy Francis after a stormy encounter at Watersheddings on April 18th. The "Airlie Birds" had triumphed by eighteen points to seven.
The game coming just two days after the Leigh match featured in the previous image proved too much for Oldham and this defeat cost them the top of the table spot, as this was the last league match of the season.

Though obviously disappointed by their narrow defeat to
Warrington, the team returned to a warm reception from the
Oldham public after the Championship final in 1955.
Left to right: Harry Ogden, Roland Barrow, Charlie Winslade,
Dick Cracknell, Alan Davies, Sid Little, Jack Keith.

County action at Watersheddings on September 26th 1955.
Lancashire's Terry O'Grady escapes the clutches of his Oldham team mate Derek Turner (playing for Yorkshire) before preparing to take on the Yorkshire full-back Jim Ledgard.

Final score: Lancashire 26 Yorkshire 10.

January 28th 1956 saw the opening of the new scoreboard for the match against Rochdale. The winning margin in the image was extended to 26 – 13 by the end of the game.

Above: John Etty - scorer of 43 tries in Oldham's Championship winning season of 1956-57. Here he is seen touching down against Blackpool Borough on March 17th 1956. Result: Oldham 37 Blackpool B. 19.

Right: Dennis Ayres - crosses the Barrow line on September 22nd 1956. Result: Oldham 45 Barrow 13.

Abe Clayton: *The first winner of the Ben Powell trophy when playing for St. Annes against Saddleworth Rangers in the 1956 Standard Cup final.*

Rangers won the match 11 – 10 but Clayton, the "Annes" loose-forward, had the singular honour of being the initial winner of the prestigious Cup final man-of-the-match award that was so named after the long serving Ferranti official Ben Powell.

227

BEN POWELL MEMORIAL TROPHY

(Sponsored by EDWARDS VEEDER CHARTERED ACCOUNTANTS)

The Oldham Amateur Rugby League were one of the forerunners in presenting 'Man of the Match' awards when Ben Powell Trophy was first presented to Ab Clayton in 1956. The trophy was presented by the local Ferranti Amat Club in remembrance of Ben Powell, who served the club for over three decades.

In the event of the draw game, the Ben Powell Trophy will still be awarded to the outstanding player in today's mat

1956	Ab. Clayton	Saint Annes	Loose Forward
1957	Dennis Flynn	Royton	Hooker
1958	Bobby Burke	Royton	Centre
1959	Brian Churm	Royton	Full Back
1960	John Yates	Saddleworth Rangers	Stand off Half
1961	Brian Clegg	Mayfield	Stand off Half
1962	Brian Jones	Saint Anne's	Full Back
1963	Tony Finan	Saddleworth Rangers	Hooker
1964	Bob McClean	Saint Mary's	Winger
1965	Brian Gartland	Saint Anne's	Stand off Half
1966	Alan Taylor	Saint Mary's	Centre
1967	Tony Lees	Saddleworth Rangers	Second Row Forward
1968	Wilf Lennigan	Saint Anne's	Centre
1969	Peter McAtee	Langworthy Juniors	Stand off Half
1970	Roy Ogden	Saint Anne's	Scrum Half
1971	Peter Moores	Saddleworth Rangers	Winger
1972	Jim Ashworth	Mayfield	Prop Forward
1973	Sid Miller	Mayfield	Scrum Half
1974	Fred Howarth	Saint Anne's	Centre
1975	Barry Edwards	Mayfield	Stand off Half
1976	Dai Evans	Saddleworth Rangers	Loose Forward
1977	Paul Kay	Saint. Anne's	Prop Forward
1978	Dave Grimbley	Saint. Anne's	Scrum Half
1979	Fred Howarth	Saint Anne's	Second row forward
1980	Shaun Gartland	Saddleworth Rangers	Scrum Half
1981	Mick Hough	Waterhead	Second Row Forward
1982	Ian Taylor	Waterhead	Centre
1983	Steve Cooper	Fitton Hill	Full Back
1984	Barry Ashworth	Mayfield	Scrum Half
1985	Graham Robinson	Shaw	Stand off Half
1986	Gary Dobbs	Waterhead	Substitue(2nd Row)
1987	Mark Lord	Saint Anne's	Centre
1988	Mick Swift	Saint Anne's	Stand off Half
1989	Paul Kay	Saint Anne's	Scrum Half
1990	Paul Graham	Saint Anne's	Second row Forward
1991	Sean Whitehead	Saddleworth Rangers	Loose Forward
1992	Roy Jewitt	Waterhead	Loose Forward
1993	Roy Jewitt	Waterhead	Loose Forward
1994	Eddie Aspin	Higginshaw	Loose Forward
1995	Paul Graham	Saint Anne's	Second Row
1996	Colin Garratt	Saddleworth Rangers	Full Back

Jack Keith, with Dick Cracknell in support, touches down against Rochdale in the Law Cup match on August 11th 1956.

Result: Oldham 34 Rochdale H. 5.

October 20th 1956.
*Oldham defeat St. Helens in the Lancashire Cup final at Wigan.
The sequence above shows John Etty scoring one of Oldham's
tries - Frank Stirrup receiving the trophy then being carried
shoulder high - The return to the civic reception and the
overjoyed Oldham supporters who turned up at the Town Hall to
welcome back their heroes.*

TWO YORKIES PARADE THE LANCASHIRE CUP!

*Yorkshiremen John Etty and Jack Keith parade the Lancashire Cup at Watersheddings
the week after the 10 - 3 triumph over St. Helens at Wigan.*

The victorious Roughyeds with the Lancashire Cup on display in the match against Keighley on October 27th 1956.
Standing: *John Etty, Griff Jenkins (coach), Don Vines, Ian Carruthers, Ken Jackson, Derek Turner, Sid Little, Charlie Winslade, Jack Keith, Bill Howard (president).*
Seated: *Bernard Ganley, Dick Cracknell, Frank Stirrup, Alan Davies, Terry O'Grady.* **Kneeling:** *Dennis Ayres, mascot, Frank Pitchford.*

Ten Oldham players are visible in this great action shot from the match against Wigan on March 30th 1957.
From left to right: Dennis Ayres, Don Vines, Vince Nestor, Frank Daley, Frank Pitchford, Ken Jackson, Charlie Winslade,
Derek Turner, Sid Little, Bernard Ganley.
For the record the other three were Dick Cracknell, Alan Davies and Jack Keith.
Result: Oldham 14 Wigan 6.

Terry O'Grady now in Wigan's colours dives over in the scoreboard corner to the dismay of his ex team-mates Sid Little, Jack Keith, Ken Jackson and Don Vines on March 30th 1957. Another bumper attendance of just under 20,000 saw Oldham eventually triumph by fourteen points to six.

April 1957 and Royton win the Standard Cup for the first time and retained the trophy for the next two seasons. Captain Billy Webb receives the cup from Oldham president, Bill Howard and Dennis Flynn (left) is pictured with the Ben Powell trophy.

The Royton team who triumphed 17 – 4 over St. Mary's.
Back Row: *W. Spencer, D. Flynn, R. Barrett, J. Worrall, C. Lomas, B. Rafferty.*
Middle Row: *W. Churm, L. Dawson, W. Webb (capt.), J. Deakin, D. Turner.*   **Front Row**: *J. Read, J. Akins.*

*Frank Pitchford releases a pass to Vince Nestor under pressure
from a Hornets' defender on April 22nd 1957.
Result: Oldham 26 Rochdale H. 12.*

The Town Hall reception May 18th 1957

Some of the scenes at the Town Hall reception given for the club after the 15 - 14 Championship final victory against Hull at Odsal Stadium, Bradford.

237

The success of winning the championship brought the crowds flocking to Watersheddings.

Here we see the queues at the turnstiles outside the ground and inside the police roll call before the match.

Sid Little crosses for a try against Warrington on September 14th 1957. In the background are Alan Jarman, Ken Jackson, Jack Keith, Don Vines and Bernard Ganley.
Result: Oldham 17 Warrington 15.

Oldham v Blackpool March 1st 1958
Back Row: *Vince Nestor, Frank Stirrup, Ron Rowbottom, Roger Dufty, Charlie Winslade, Frank Daley, Don Vines.*
Front Row: *Frank Pitchford, Dennis Ayres, Dick Cracknell, John Etty, John Noon, Ian Carruthers.*

Bernard Ganley tackles Dave Bolton into touch. This was the match that broke Oldham's run of fourteen consecutive victories over Wigan. It was a 3rd round Challenge Cup tie, which as you can see was played before a massive crowd of 23,000 spectators on March 8th 1958. Wigan duly went on to win the cup against Workington Town in the final.
Result: Oldham 0 Wigan 8.

1958

Ike Southward is tackled by John Etty on April 26 1958.

A year later Southward would be an Oldham player and Etty would leave to join Wakefield.

Result:
Oldham 10 Workington 8.

May 3rd 1958 and having finished top of the league table it was thought that the Championship would be retained, but fourth placed Hull ruined the Roughyeds' dream with a twenty points to eight victory at Watersheddings in the play-off semi-final.
Here Frank Pitchford can be seen tackling Cyril Sykes with Dennis Ayres, Dick Cracknell, Sid Little and Roger Dufty in attendance.
Result: Oldham 8 Hull 20.

Cyril Sykes evades Bernard Ganley to score in the Championship play-off semi-final.

TOUR REPRESENTATIVES

Club president Bill Howard presents international caps to:
Ken Jackson, Alan Davies, Sid Little, Derek Turner and Bernard Ganley for their appearance against France.

Although Little and Turner were initially selected for the 1958 tour only Davies, Jackson and Pitchford would eventually make the trip.

Alan Davies

Ken Jackson

Frank Pitchford

Above: Bernard Ganley points to the number 224 the figure that was the total of all the goals he kicked in the 1957-58 season including those in representative games and the Law cup.

Above left: Club physiotherapist, Frank Navesey, massages Charlie Winslade in the treatment room as Derek Turner looks on.

Left: Three Leigh born, scrum-halves discuss tactics over a cup of tea in the pavilion. Left to right - Frank Stirrup, Frank Pitchford and Brian Hatherall.

THE GOLDEN GOAL

Left: Bernard Ganley slots home the record breaking goal number 200 against Hunslet at Watersheddings on 12th April 1958.
This was the first time anyone had reached the double century in a single season.
Right: Photographed on the now overgrown bowling green, in front of the dilapidated former bowling pavilion.

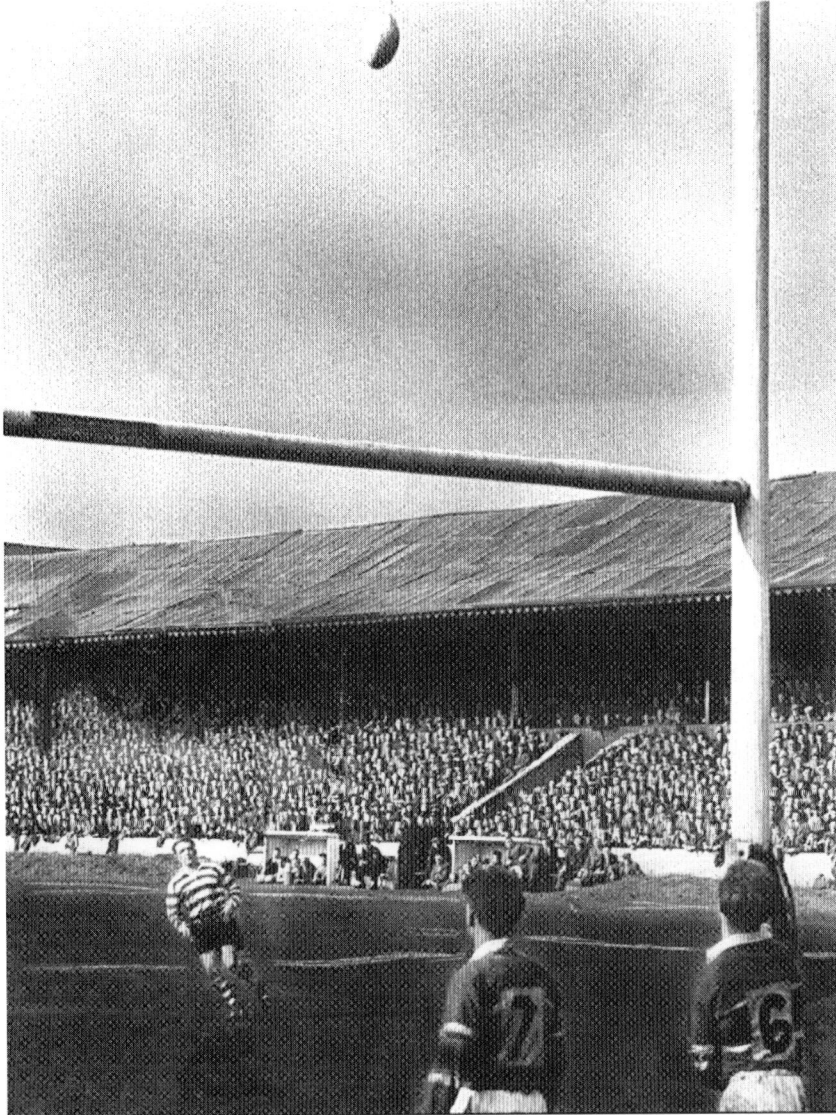

1958

The Watersheddings stand under construction in summer 1958.

The picture on the left shows Roger Dufty scoring in the final game in the 1957-58 season against Hull, immediately after which construction on the new stand commenced.

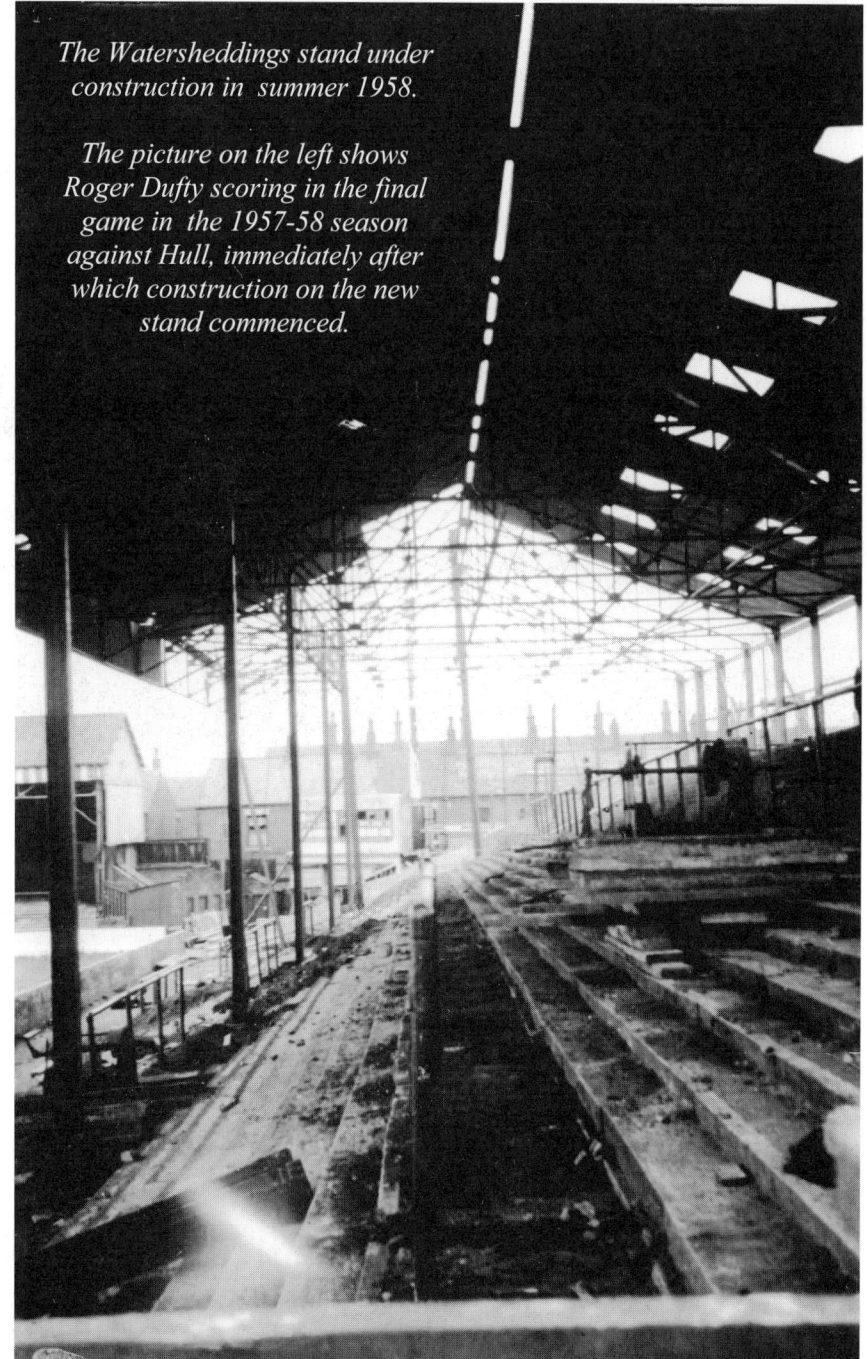

The first match of the 1958-59 season against Halifax on August 19th saw the opening of the new stand at the Watersheddings end.

The action on the left shows Briers the Halifax full-back attempting a penalty goal towards the new stand.

Below: The sequence shows Vince Nestor breaking clear only to be hauled down within inches of the Halifax line.

Oldham won the match 21 – 10 before a crowd of 12,319.

Two Watersheddings tries for Oldham's "prince of centres" Alan Davies.
Above: Davies turns to go under the posts in the match against Whitehaven on August 30th 1958.
Right: It's Hunslet on the receiving end as he leaves a posse of defenders in his wake on September 12th 1959.

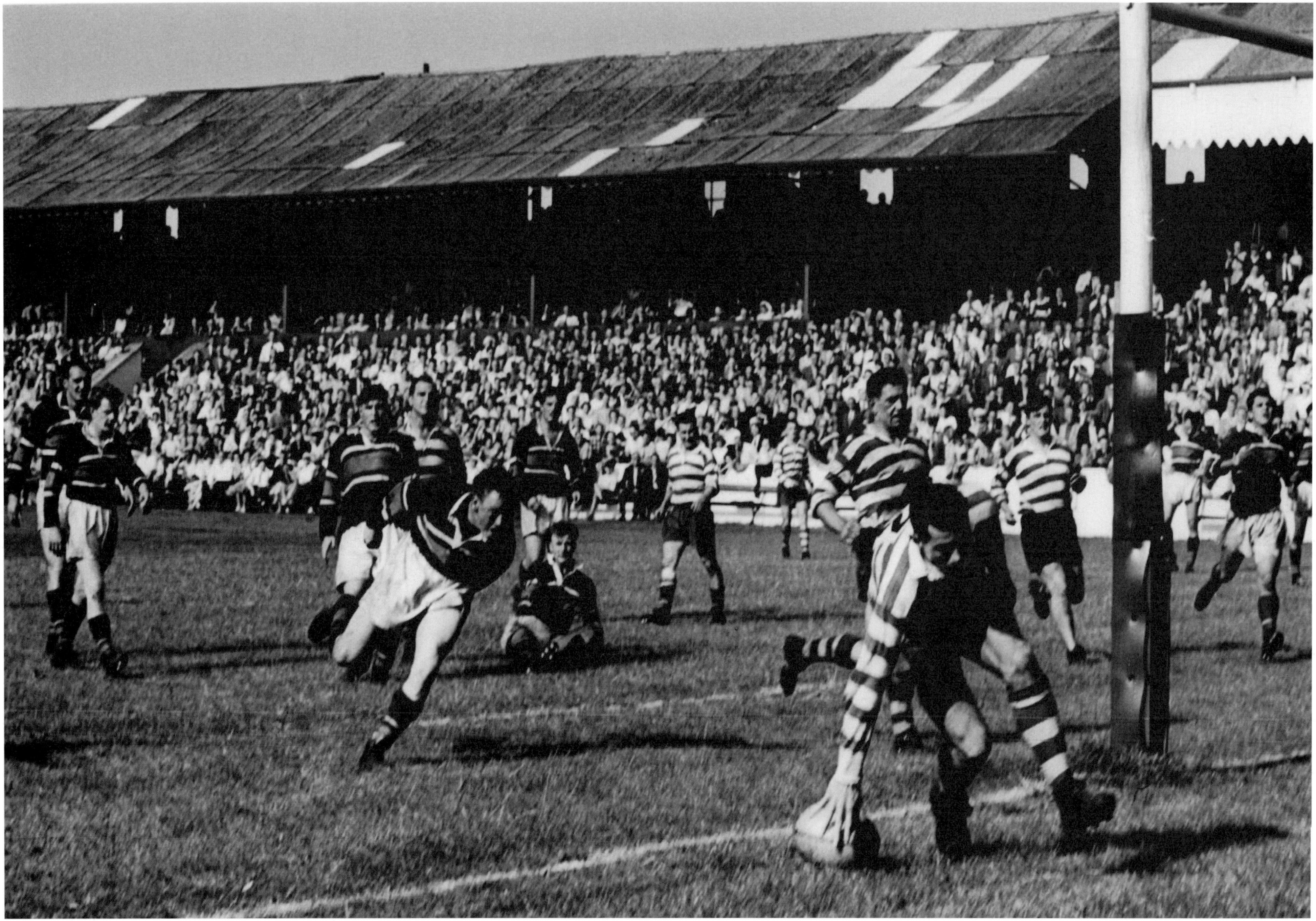

1959

Oldham established a then club-record points total of 67 in the match against Liverpool City on April 4th 1959. This included four tries each for Alan Kellett and Dick Cracknell and 14 goals for Bernard Ganley, a club record for goals in a match which still stands in 2010.
Left: Ken Jackson crosses the line.
Below: Vince Nestor cuts through the Liverpool defence.

October 31st 1959: Geoff Robinson foils a Barrow attack. Oldham scored only two tries but seven goals from the "maestro" Bernard Ganley tipped the match in Oldham's favour. Result: Oldham 20 Barrow 9.

Two record signings!
Geoff Robinson and Ike Southward pictured at a training
session shortly after Robinson's arrival in August 1959.

Robinson was signed from Whitehaven for £9,000 which
was then a record for a forward.

Southward came from Workington in March of the same
year for a fee of £10,650 which represented the highest
transfer deal of any player at that time.

Right: September 8th 1959 and that's the Halifax winger Johnny
Freeman being forced down by Des McKeown with Vince Nestor and
Bernard Ganley on hand if required.
Result: Oldham 21 Halifax 17.

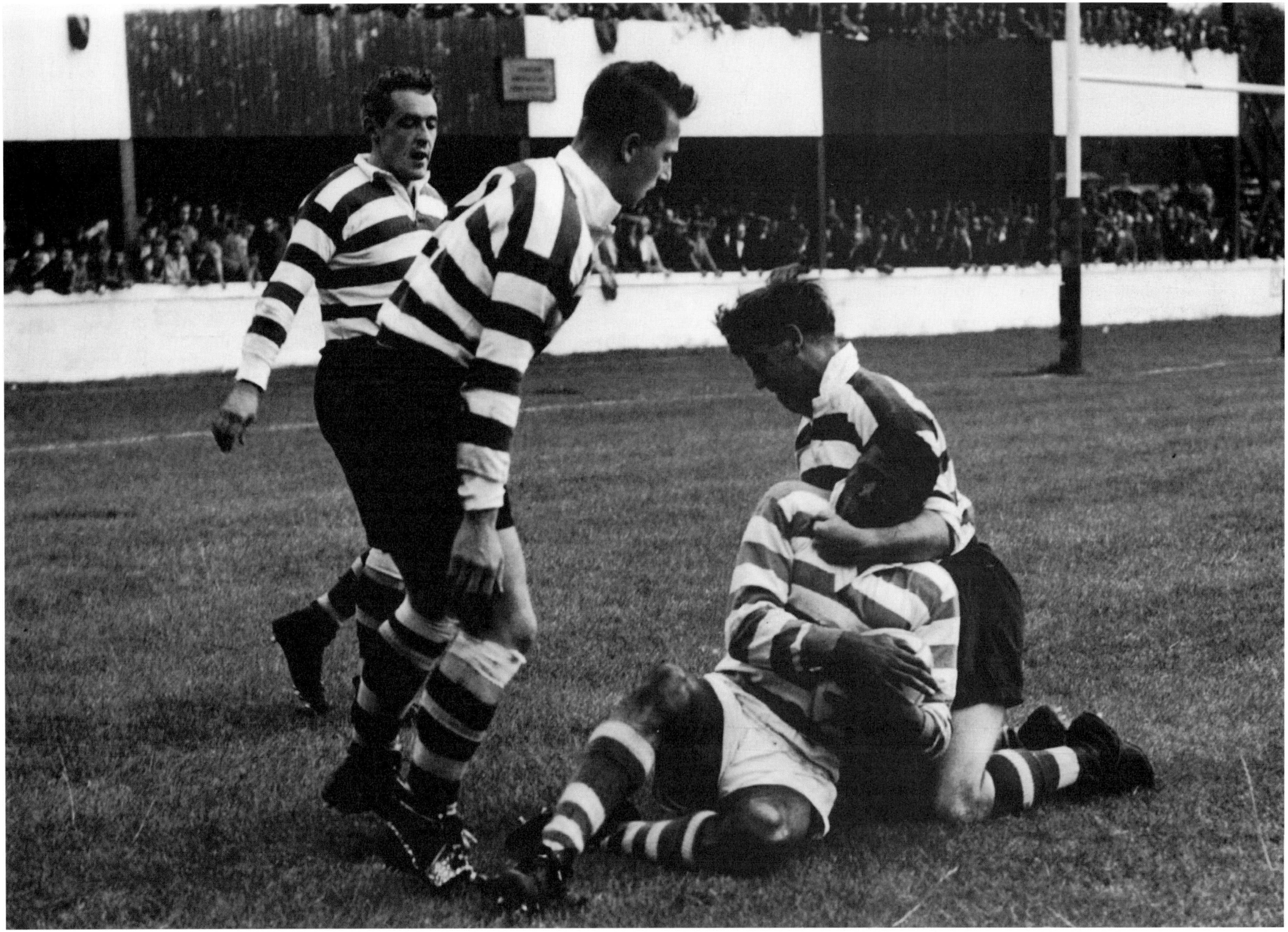

Des McKeown, Geoff Sims and Frank Pitchford halt the progress of a Blackpool opponent on November 14th 1959.
Result: Oldham 34 Blackpool B. 5.

Brian Lord dives over to score against Salford on February 6th 1960.
Brian was no stranger to the dramatic score as you will see in the following pages.
Result: Oldham 20 Salford 15.

Training session 1960.

Two tries against the Barrow amateur team Walney Central in the Challenge Cup
second round on February 27th 1960.
Above: Charlie Winslade touches down with Roger Dufty in support.
Right: Ike Southward scores one of his six tries in this match.
Result: Oldham 54 Walney Central 5.

Early March 1960 .
Reserve forwards, Alf Mumberson and Dick Smith, are called up for first team training
ahead of the 3rd round cup-tie against Bramley, as cover for the injured Ken Jackson.

Above: Fisticuffs! Tempers flare in the Challenge Cup 3rd round against Bramley on March 9th 1960.
Vince Nestor touches down for one of his two tries that settled the match.
Result: Oldham 8 Bramley 2.

Right: The reward for the narrow victory over Bramley was a semi-final against Hull played at Station Road, Swinton.

Although hopes were high amongst the Oldham supporters, it wasn't to be for the Roughyeds and it was the "Airlie Birds" who progressed to Wembley.

The photo shows Geoff Robinson and Dick Smith bringing down Peter Whiteley.
Result: Hull 12 Oldham 9.

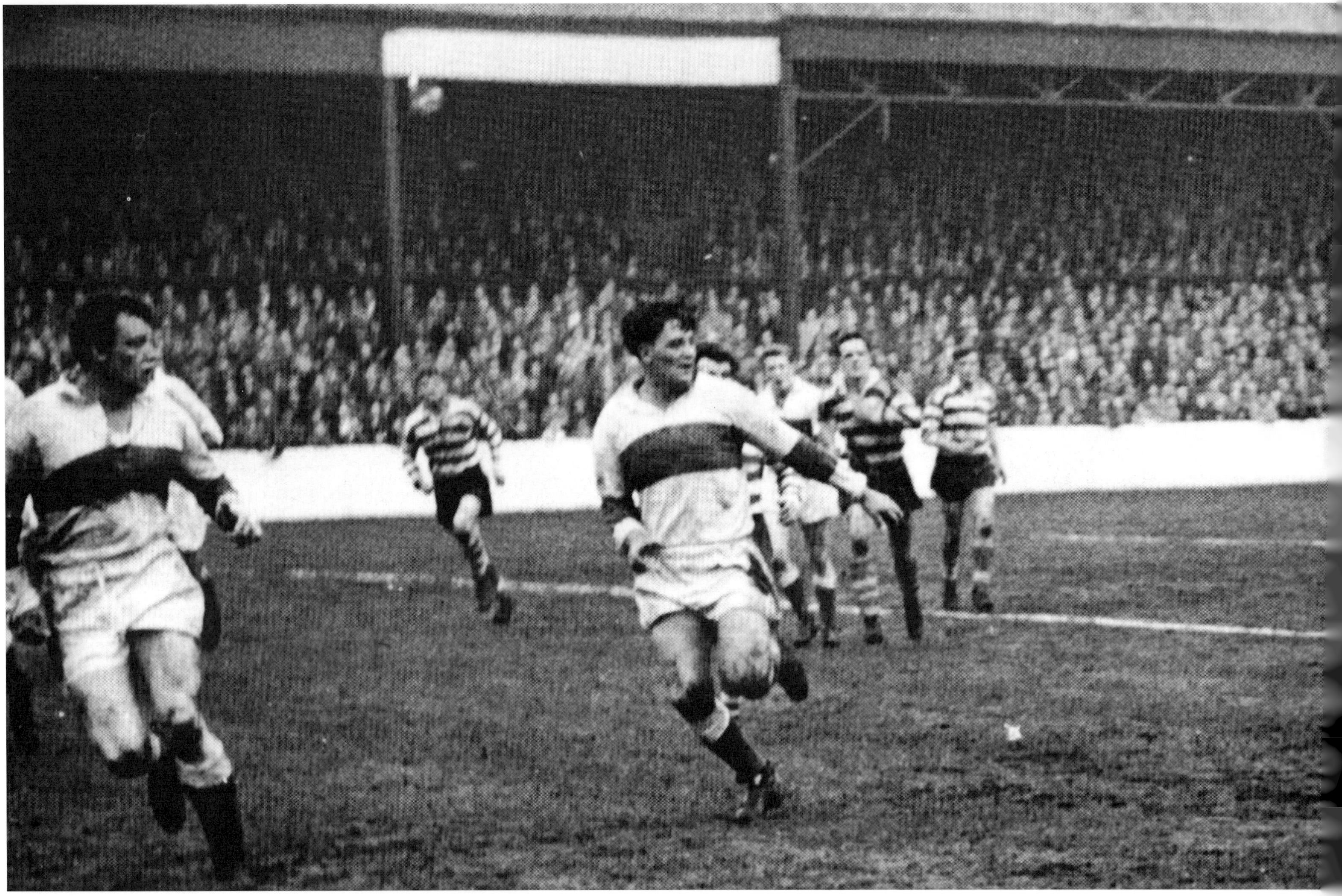

Johnny Noon in action against St Helens on April 26th 1960
Result: Oldham 2 St. Helens 10.

Alan Kellett on the move against St. Helens on August 13th 1960.
Result: Oldham 16 St. Helens 4.

Alan Kellett goes over for a try against Rochdale on September 16th 1961.
Other Oldham players: Geoff Robinson, Roger Dufty, Bill Payne, Len McIntyre and John Rae.
Result: Oldham 53 Rochdale H. 9.

Alf Mumberson is brought down within sight of the Warrington line by Brian Bevan with
John Rae and John Noon in support on October 21st 1961.
Result: Oldham 35 Warrington 5.

The Oldham team that defeated Whitehaven 45 – 10 on December 2nd 1961.
Back Row: L. McIntyre, P. Smethurst, D. Parker, J. Rae, P. Goddard, W. Payne, B. Lord.
Front Row: W. Patterson, G. Sims, J. Noon, F. Pitchford, A. Kellett, M. Bird.

Action from the 1st round Challenge Cup tie against Hull on February 10th 1962.
Geoff Robinson, Brian Lord and Keith Holden halt the progress of the Hull centre while John Rae looks on.
Result: Oldham 32 Hull 16.

Good Friday, 1962 and St. Annes claim the Standard Cup for the first time. The "green and golds" triumphed by way of a 17 – 9 victory over their perennial rivals, Saddleworth Rangers.
Back Row: Ogden, Thackeray, Murray, Sexton, Quinn, J. Walker, Leach.
Front Row: Taylor, Patterson, W. Walker, Gartland, Smith, Jones, Tully.

Mike Bird goes to ground against Swinton on April 24th 1962.
Other Oldham players: Geoff Sims, John Noon, Dave Parker, Keith Holden.
Result: Oldham 8 Swinton 15.

Another action shot from the match against Swinton on April 24th 1962.
The referee and touch judge intervene as tempers flare!

*Oldham v Huddersfield October 13th 1962. Alf Mumberson completes
a tackle with Geoff Sims and Peter Smethurst at the ready.
Result: Oldham 9 Huddersfield 8.*

Snowy training session in early 1963.

The Oldham squad in training in the week leading up to the Wigan cup-tie on April 6th:
Left to right: J. Noon, L. McIntyre, W. Patterson, J. Donovan, T. Simms, R. Fisher,
A. Kellett, A. Mumberson, G. Robinson, P. Smethurst.

Nothing like a cup quarter final to pack the terraces and it's Wigan again on April 6th 1963. Another 23,000 crowd saw Oldham go down 18 – 0. Here we see John Donovan attempting to cut between Frank Collier, Stan McLeod and Frank Pitchford (then with Wigan) as Ray Fisher looks on.

Left: Charlie Bott, the Oldham prop-forward taking on the Whitehaven defence on September 18th 1963.
Result: Oldham 35 Whitehaven 4.

A rare try for Charlie three days later against Barrow on September 21st 1963.
Result: Oldham 35 Barrow 8.

Roughyeds' captain Frank Dyson receives a Mackeson silver tankard from the Whitbread regional manager, under the watchful eye of club official Harry Goodwin.
Oldham topped the league scoring averages in October 1963 to secure the honour.

1963

A superb action photograph of Brian Lord diving over for a try against Doncaster on October 12th 1963.

This was the Don's first ever visit to Watersheddings when the rampant Roughyeds ran out 45 - 13 winners.

Players officials and back-room staff enjoy a drink at the Oldham Rugby Christmas party in 1963.

A piece of rugby league history, as Peter Smethurst scores for Oldham against Blackpool Borough despite the attentions of Brian Bevan.

This was to be the last senior game for the great "Bev" on February 22nd 1964.

Result: Oldham 18 Blackpool B. 5.

John Donovan takes on the Barrow defence in the match at Watersheddings on March 21st 1964.
Result: Oldham 32 Barrow 5.

St. Mary's beat Langworthy by two points to nil in a tough Standard Cup final on Good Friday, 1964.

Pre-season trial match played on August 8th 1964.

1964

Oldham v Swinton August 29th 1964.
Right: John Donovan makes a tackle with Harry Major and Jack Pycroft in attendance.

Below: Malcolm Price puts in a kick as Ken Wilson and Jack Pycroft prepare to give chase.

Result: Oldham 13 Swinton 2.

Above: Joe Collins gets a pass away to Jim McCormack (unseen) who in turn puts Geoff Sims over for a try.

Right: McCormack and Collins congratulate Sims after the touchdown to the approval of the Herbert Street side terrace supporters.

Action from the match against Liverpool City on September 12th 1964 Result: Oldham 42 Liverpool C. 5.

Oldham v Huddersfield March 27th 1965 and three different views of Joe Collins.
First - scoring one of his two tries in the twelve points to two win
Second – pulling off a tackle
Third – taking a tackle.

Rugby special leaving West Street for Watersheddings on match day.

Floodlights were installed at Watersheddings in October 1965. Here club president Bert Jones and secretary John Stringer can be seen overseeing the installation and the Herbert Street "Popular" side with the newly installed pylons.

The first floodlit match took place on October 20th when the Great Britain under 24s side defeated the French by twelve points to five.

Bert Summerscales was officially connected with the club for 40 years until his retirement as secretary in 1965.

Elected to the committee in 1925, he was honorary treasurer from April 1939 to June 1946: honorary secretary from 1941 to 1946 and full time secretary from 1946 until 1965.

Oldham v Wigan September 30th 1966.
Back Row: *Geoff Fletcher, Bob Irving, Ken Wilson, Alf Mumberson, Mick Mooney, Charlie Bott, John Donovan.*
Front Row: *Tommy Warburton, Brian Curry, Terry Dolly, Trevor Simms, Peter Smethurst, Jim McCormack, Kevin Taylor, Stan McLeod, Tom Canning.*
(Dolly and Mooney were the substitutes and Bott was 16th man.)
Result: Oldham 15 Wigan 16.

Left: Billboards advertise rugby league at Watersheddings with games against Huddersfield and Halifax in March 1967.

*Below action from the match against Huddersfield on March 11th.
Result: Oldham 9 Huddersfield 4.*

*Right:
Terry Dolly takes a tackle
watched by Trevor Buckley and
Geoff Fletcher.*

291

Tom Canning attempts to bring down Eric Ashton watched by team mates, Mike Elliott, Alan Ogden and Geoff Shelton on September 30th 1967.
Result: Oldham 13 Wigan 17.

Three internal views of the social club opened in 1967. The club was prepared to be ready for use to coincide with the visit of the Australian tourists on November 11th.

Left: The main lounge.

Below left: The concert room.

Below right: The "gentlemen's" room.

1968

Oldham R.L.F.C. committee in the late 1960s.
Back Row: *A. Parker, F. Buckley, A. Wormald, P. Carter, J. Stringer, J. Burke, L. Eyre, S. McDonough.*
Front Row: *W. Howard, A. Campbell, H. Jones, K. Fisher, J. Errock.*

Wilf Briggs was signed to beat the 1968 Cup deadline from Leigh in an exchange deal that saw Tommy Warburton going to Hilton Park. Oldham also picked up £5,000.
Briggs was an excellent try poacher and scored 44 touchdowns in just 73 matches for Oldham.
Also in the photograph is Kevin Taylor who also had a knack for crossing the whitewash and topped the Oldham try scorers twice in the 1960s.
A remarkable achievement for a hooker!

1968

The Oldham Chronicle Cup was introduced for a pre-season friendly away against Blackpool Borough in 1967.

The following year the match played at Watersheddings on August 10th saw the Oldham debut of Phil Larder and resulted in a 37 – 27 victory for the Roughyeds.

Captain, Geoff Fletcher is seen here receiving the cup. Also in the photograph are Wilf Briggs, Kevin Taylor and Ken Wilson.

The Oldham team that defeated Widnes 17 – 9 at Watersheddings on October 19th 1968.
Back Row: *Charlie McCourt, Ken Wilson, Jim McCormack, Bob Irving, Phil Larder, Dennis Maders, Mike Elliott.*
Front Row: *Ged Smith, Wilf Briggs, Tom Canning, Geoff Fletcher, Derek Whitehead, Kevin Taylor, Martin Murphy, Colin Smith.*

OLDHAM FOOTBALL CLUB SOCIAL CLUB
Notice to Members

COMING ATTRACTIONS

NOON TOMORROW !

ALL STAR WRESTLING

DON VINES v. THE OUTLAW

— PLUS SUPPORTING BOUT —

Tickets on sale to Members in the Social Club - 5/- each

TICKETS ALSO ON SALE 5/- FOR THE FABULOUS

THE SECOND CITY SOUND SHOW

— with All Star supporting Acts —

THURSDAY, 10th OCTOBER, commencing 8 p.m.

This will be a knock-out Show — Don't miss !

One of the attractions at the social club was wrestling bouts. Here we see ex-Roughyed favourite Don Vines in October 1968, billed to take on The Outlaw!

Left and above: Don Vines wrestler and rugby player.

Below: The Outlaw.

A clearly painful looking Jim Crellin is helped into the dug-out by Charlie McCourt and Jimmy Howarth in January 1969 watched with concern by coach, Gerry Helme.

Langworthy celebrate in time honoured style on the pavilion steps after winning the 1969 Standard Cup final against St. Annes.

Captain, David Snell holds the Cup and Peter McAtee shows off the Ben Powell trophy for which he was the unanimous choice as man-of-the-match.

A fine action shot of Wilf Briggs diving on the ball to score one of a hat-trick of tries in the 41 – 10 defeat of Keighley on September 6th 1969.

*Martin Murphy and Jimmy Howarth enter into the spirit of a
Radio Caroline road show at the social club in the late 1960s.*

The greyhound track was the subject of a take-over by the St Helens business man Joe Pickavance in April 1970.
In the deal the Oldham club received a down payment of two years rental at £20 a week (£2080).

TOUR REPRESENTATIVE

Bob Irving

A model of consistency during his entire spell with the Roughyeds, Bob Irving was a speedy second-row forward whose selection for the 1970 tour was all the more remarkable for it coinciding with a very poor season for the Oldham club.

Oldham v Barrow December 19th 1970.
Back Row: *Ray Fletcher, Ray Clark, Frank Walker, Bob Irving, Jim Reynolds, Arthur Daley, Ken Wilson, Cliff Sayer.*
Front Row: *Kevin Taylor, Martin Murphy, Graham Starkey, Phil Larder, Terry Garrett.*
Kneeling: *Ged Smith, mascot, Tommy Davies.*
Result: Oldham 13 Barrow 2.

Martin Murphy cuts through the Featherstone defence as Norman Hodgkinson attempts to support the attack on October 2nd 1971. Result: Oldham 17 Featherstone R. 21.

THE AMERICAN DREAM

Above: American rugby union players, Chris Machado and Sam Moore, from the Peninsula Ramblers club in San Jose, California, along with John Alchin, Brian Grace and Oldham officials Jack Bowden and Kevin Wilkinson. Moore and Machado had a brief spell with the Roughyeds in 1971.

Left: Moore and Machado with a young admirer.

1971

It was the turn of Saddleworth Rangers to lift the Standard
Cup in 1971 with a 20 – 8 victory over St. Annes.

In the photograph the team show off the Cup on the pavilion
steps with coach John Noon in the centre. Peter Moore was
the proud recipient of the Ben Powell trophy.

An exhibition of Oldham memorabilia took place at the St. James Conservative Club on Ripponden Road.

The photograph shows from left to right:
Ex-Oldham players Edgar Brooks and Norman Pugh, Hubert Lockwood the chairman of the Rugby League and referee Billy Thompson of Huddersfield.

The Oldham "B" (under 19s) team in 1972:

Back Row: D. Smith, T. Langham, R. O'Mahoney, P. Deakin, S. Mykyta, J. Glover, G. Byrom, B. Byrom.
Front Row: S. Bottom, G. Lyons, F. Royales, J. Kenyon, S. Whitmore, I. Radcliffe, T. Hope.

1972

The Standard Cup left town for Rochdale after Mayfield defeated Waterhead 18 – 3 in the 1972 final.

Amongst the players pictured are:
S. Miller, J. Power, J. Haigh, J. Swain, K. Knox, B. Edwards, B. Ashworth, J. Mills, M. McGuigan, A. Butterworth, J. Bate, J. Dawson, H. Leach and Jim Ashworth the captain who also picked up the Ben Powell trophy.

A try for Bob Irving against Hull on September 10th 1972.
Also in the photograph:Chris O'Brien, Phil Larder, Kevin Taylor and Cliff Hill.

Martin Murphy pictured above provided the highlight of the 1972-73 season when he won the BBC "Try of the Season" award for a marvellous effort in the televised match at Leigh on December 5th 1972.

1972

Frank Foster, with Kevin Taylor and Geoff Munro in support, looks to off-load, in the Law Cup game against Rochdale on August 12th 1972 and can be seen later picking up the trophy from local R.L. historian Tom Webb after a narrow 18 – 16 victory for the Roughyeds.

*More action form the 1972 Law Cup game.
Mick Siddall and Tommy Davies combine to bring down a
Rochdale opponent.*

*Ready for the next match!
Jimmy Howarth makes sure the kit is spic and span!*

1973

Two images from a sparsely attended game against St Helens on December 8th 1973.
Attendance: 2,408.
Result: Oldham 12 St Helens 11.

Left: Mick McCone dives over for a try in the 30 – 20 defeat of Leigh, on December 23rd 1973.
Other Oldham players left to right: John Blair, Tony Peters, Brian Gregory, Fred Hall, Bill McCracken and Mike Elliott.

Right: More action from the game against Leigh in December 1973.

Geoff Munro moves in to stifle a Leigh attack under the scrutiny of Tony Peters, Brian Gregory and referee Gerry Kershaw.

January 1974 and kit-man Jimmy Howarth (temporarily raised to constable) exchanges some banter with the spectators.

```
            P R O G R A M M E
         CHARITY FOOTBALL MATCH
             PROCEEDS TO

    OLDHAM SOCIETY FOR MENTALLY HANDICAPPED
         CHILDREN (GATEWAY CLUB)

                  ON

    SUNDAY, 19TH MAY, 1974.   K.O. 2.45 p.m.

                  AT

       OLDHAM RUGBY LEAGUE FOOTBALL CLUB
              WATERSHEDDINGS

    ALL STAR XI      versus     OLDHAM ATHLETIC &
                                   OLDHAM RUGBY

    The Dooley Family           Eddie Barton
    Stu Francis                 Ronnie Blair
    Carl Denver                 Jimmy Brannigan
    Dave Berry                  Ian Buckley
    Tommy Banks                 Steve Cox
    Derek Quinn                 Mike Elliott
    Cannon and                  Fred Hall
    Ball                        Ian Holland
                                Phil Larder
                                Dick Mulvaney
                                Martin Murphy
                                Chris Ogden
                                Andy Sweeney
                                Maurice Whittle

    COMMENTATOR:  MR. BERNARD MANNING

    REFEREE:      MR. SAM SHEPHERD

    LINESMEN:     MR. ERIC LEACH AND
                  MR. GORDON PRIESTLEY

    FOOTBALL      MR. JOHN V. SHEIDON,
    DONATED BY:   JUNCTION INN, DENSHAW.

    Admission by Programme        Price 10p.
```

O.S.M.H.C. GATEWAY CLUB

Local show business and sports personalities got together for this charity football match in aid of the Oldham Gateway Club on May 19th 1974.

Below left; Bernard Manning.
Below right: Cannon and Ball.

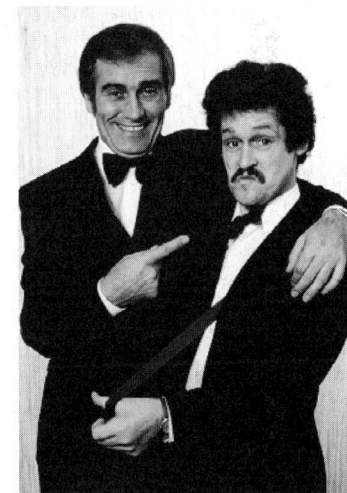

TOUR REPRESENTATIVE

Terry Clawson
A goal kicking prop-forward, Clawson played in all three tests against the touring Australians in 1973 and in four of the six tests on the 1974 tour to Australia and New Zealand.
(left): Scoring for Oldham against Whitehaven in October 1973. (right): Playing for Great Britain against Australia.

Fred Hall in action against Hull on October 12th 1974.
Result: Oldham 10 Hull 5.

1975

Coach, Jim Challinor directs a session on the training ground in February 1975, prior to a Challenge Cup tie at Rochdale.

Back Row:
Keith Ashcroft,
Bob Welding,
Johnny Farrell,
Eddie Barton,
Brian Hughes,
Mike Elliott,
Tony Wainwright,
Fred Hall,
Phil Larder,
Jim Reynolds.

Front Row:
John Blair,
David Treasure,
Kevin Taylor,
Dickie Brown.

Action from the Challenge Cup quarter final against
Widnes on March 9th 1975.

Over 11,000 turned up to watch Oldham put in a great
effort before going down to the eventual cup winners.
Result: Oldham 4 Widnes 10.

TUG WILSON

SOUVENIR PROGRAMME

1963

1975

OLDHAM
v
ENGLAND

April 22nd 1975   Kick off 7-30

Programme   10p

Popular prop-forward Ken "Tug" Wilson was granted a benefit match in April 1975 when Oldham took on an England XIII.

England had too much for the Roughyeds and ran out easy winners 27 - 5.

He played in 321 first team matches for Oldham between 1963 and 1973.

Below: Ken in action against Wigan on September 29th 1972.

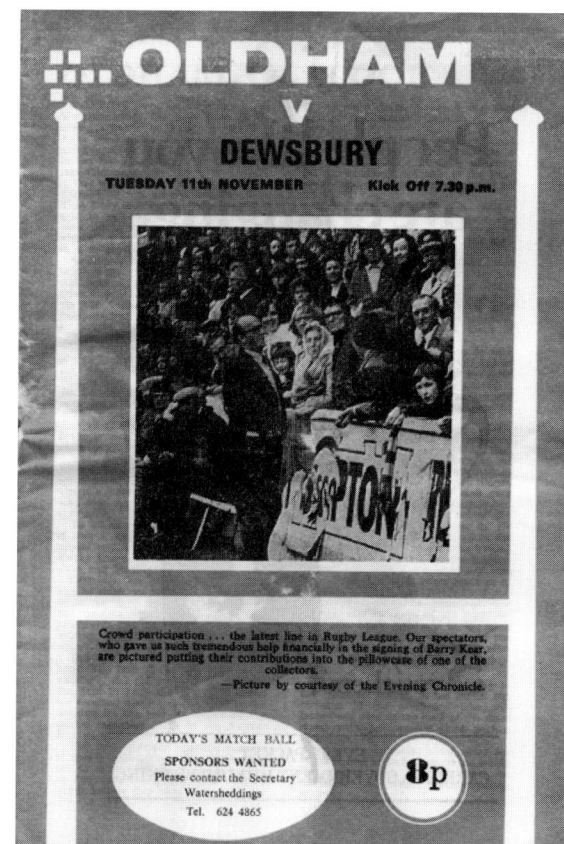

Terry Ramshaw drives into the Dewsbury defence on November 2nd 1975.
One of the Oldham tries that day was scored by Barry Kear who the club signed, after a trial
period, with the help of contributions by supporters gathered in a "pillow case" collection
held at half-time in the match. The moment is captured on the front of the match programme
when Dewsbury visited Watersheddings again nine days later.
Result: Oldham 15 Dewsbury 6.

Oldham and Featherstone players observe a minutes silence for ex Oldham forward Billy Moore before the start of the match on April 4th 1976.

Captain John Hammond holds aloft the Lancashire Shield after the "A" team players' victory over Salford in April 1976. Most of the team have managed to squeeze into this picture. The players on duty that day were:
Gordon Pollard, Geoff Munro, Mick Siddall, Keith Jackson, Steve Lund, John Patterson, John Hammond,
Ray Hicks, Roger O'Mahoney, Ian Taylor, Warren Ryans, Paul Starbuck, Jim Reynolds. Subs: Steve Herbert and Gareth Owen.

October 1976: a meeting of the Ladies Centenary Committee - left to right: Joyce Pilkington, Linda Collinge, Vera Hough, Faye Bowden, Alice Collinge and Ann Potter.

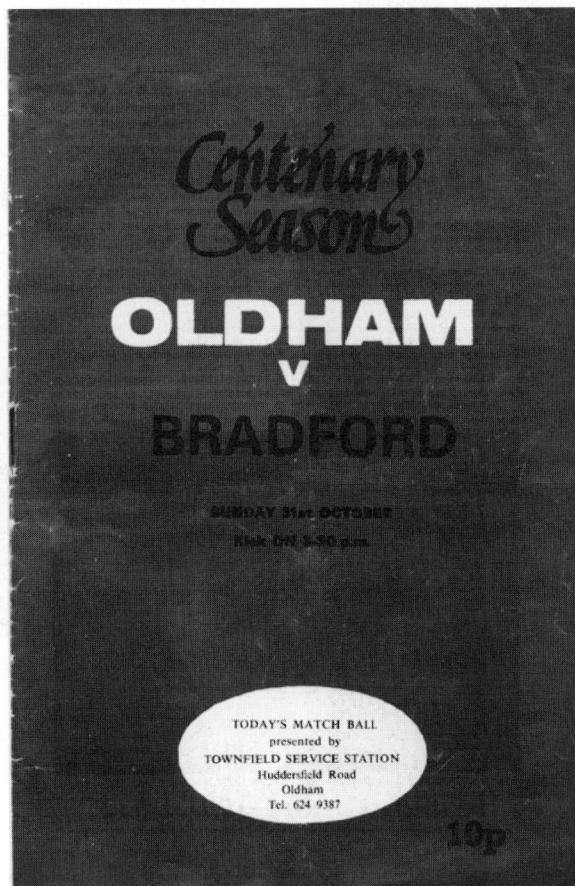

Oldham celebrated the centenary of the formation of the club with the match against Bradford on October 31st 1976.

Shown above: (left) The Mayor, Councillor Christopher McCall, shaking hands with young Martin Hall the Oldham mascot in the presence of club captain Martin Murphy and chairman Arthur Walker.
(middle) The special centenary programme.
(right) The pre-match seven-a-side schoolboys teams being presented with medals from the club vice-chairman John Hall.

Scrum-half Alan Bates plus Oldham props Fred Hall and Brian Hughes can be seen peering over the scrum as referee Billy Thompson awards Oldham a penalty. December 26th 1977.

Inset: Uri Stondin suffers a broken jaw in the fiery derby encounter with Rochdale on Boxing Day 1977. Result: Oldham 5 Rochdale H. 14.

1978

The Oldham Supporters' Club team celebrate in the social club after becoming the Manchester area quiz champions in January 1978.

Left to right: Ian Pilkington, Alan Burke, Kevin McDonough and Keith Burley.

"The loneliness of the single-handed groundsman!"

Dennis Truelove conducts a one man snow shifting operation before the cup-tie against Doncaster on February 26th 1978.

A pram-race organised in aid of the Phil Larder benefit fund on May 29th 1979.
The 3 mile course, centred around Watersheddings and Huddersfield Road (including 15 pubs!), featured some celebrity entries.
One of the ladies' teams, dressed in the Oldham kit, assemble on the car park outside Watersheddings.

Another team passing by the junction between Ripponden Road and Huddersfield Road.
Other teams included a couple dressed in bandages who, when the race was over, were revealed to be senior referees Mick Naughton and Robin Whitfield, and a team from Saddleworth School containing Larder himself and team mate Eddie Barton.

Fred Howarth, holds up the Ben Powell trophy after the drawn match between St. Annes and Mayfield on Good Friday 1979. Fred became the first player to win the honour twice having already picked up the trophy in 1974. Unfortunately for the Saints, Mayfield won the replay.

Lord Pilkington opens the refurbished pavilion in May 1979 with club officials Keith Broadbent, Jack Bowden and Ray Hatton in attendance.

335

LIKE FATHER LIKE SON!
BEN POWELL TROPHY WINNERS

Following on from father Brian's success in 1965 (above) for St. Annes, son Shaun made it a Gartland family double when he picked up the Ben Powell trophy while playing for Saddleworth Rangers in the 1980 Standard Cup final, ironically against St. Annes.

Oldham captain Paddy Kirwan holds up the Colt's Championship trophy in May 1980.

Waterhead pose on the pavilion steps after a narrow 9 – 7 victory over Saddleworth Rangers in 1981 that secured them the Standard Cup for the first time. Coach Ken Wilson can be seen on the far left of the photograph.

Victorious captain Ian Taylor receives the cup from Terry Flanagan and Mick Hough holds on to the Ben Powell trophy, the first player from 'head to win the award.

Ladies Rugby at Watersheddings

"Ladies Rugby at Watersheddings". Referee Billy Thompson is the man in the middle as the ladies of Waterhead and Oldham pose for a photograph in May 1981. The Oldham ladies triumphed by eighteen point to nil aided by a hat-trick from winger Sylvia Brezneck.

The Oldham ladies' team photographed in October 1981 with coaching assistant, Paul Collinge, and coach, Joe Warburton, at the back.
Back Row: *Alice Collinge (manager), Sarah Tolson, Kath Dowd, Anne Doleman, Suzanne Gluvons, Melanie Hilton, Sue Pullen, Leslie Warburton, Lara Hunt.*
Front Row: *Jackie Warburton, Dawn Riley, Teresa Winterbottom, Dawn Williams, Jean Warburton.*

High-profile rugby union converts Bob Mordell and Adrian Alexander parade the second division Championship trophy around Watersheddings after the final game against Workington Town on May 9th 1982.

The team celebrate in the dressing room with the second division
Championship trophy after the victory over Workington.

1982

January 1982 - Brian Lawrence, manager of the Oldham greyhound stadium,
photographed with the track's new "all-sand" surface in the background.
Further in the distance one can see the pavilion and the Watersheddings' main stand.

Andy Goodway and Terry Flanagan receive their international caps from club chairman Ray Hatton.

1984

Action from the infamous match against Leigh on January 8th 1984.

Below: Mick Morgan takes on the Leigh defence with Mike Taylor, Ian Birkby, Terry Flanagan, Craig Coyle and Des Foy looking on.

Right: Paddy Kirwan and Jimmy Hornby bring down Des Drummond.

This was the game abandoned in the second-half for fighting after 58 minutes. It wasn't pretty, but it wasn't that bad either.

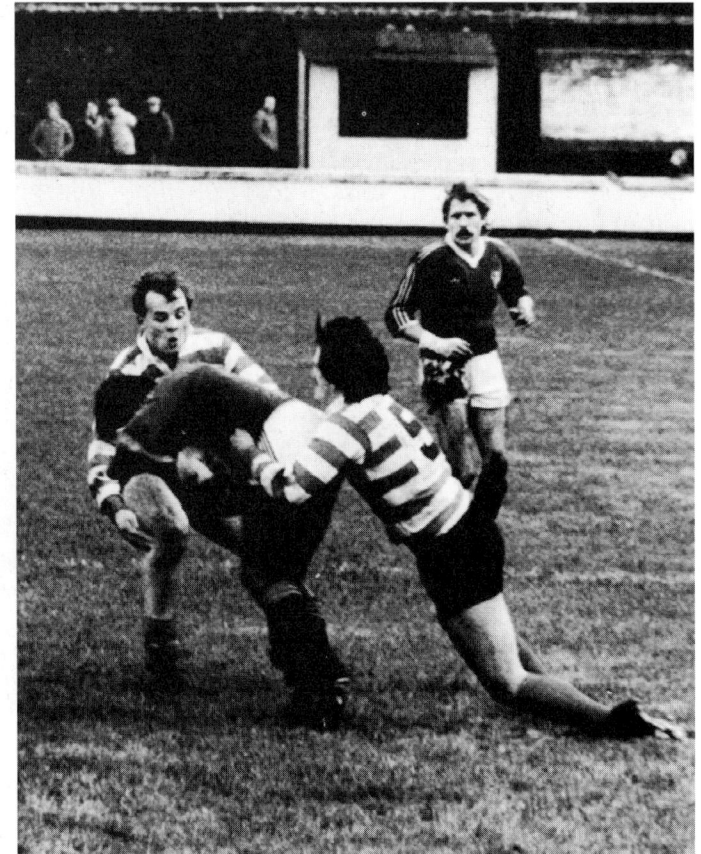

When the match was abandoned Leigh were leading 26 - 14 but in the subsequent replay played on March 11th, Oldham won 13 - 10.

TOUR REPRESENTATIVES

Oldham first team squad 1984.
***Back Row**: J. Watkins, A. Platt, G. Vigo, M. Worrall.*
***Middle Row**: F. Barrow, M. Morgan, W. Jones, G. Pollard, A. McEwan, M. Coombes, P. Smethurst, A. Bonelle.*
***Front Row**: T. Flanagan, D. Foy, S. Littler, R. Ashton, A. McCurrie, A. Goodway, C. Willis, P. Lowndes, P. Kirwan.*
*Five players: **Worrall, Flanagan, Foy, Ashton** and **Goodway** were selected for the 1984 tour to Australia and New Zealand.*
A record for the club.

Des Foy takes a pass from the grounded Jimmy Hornby in the match against Hunslet on September 2nd 1984.
Result: Oldham 32 Hunslet 10.

"The Big Switch On"
Oldham's new floodlights are used for
the first time in the drawn match
against Leeds on March 3rd 1985.
This image shows how the pitch used to
slope down to the right corner of the
Hutchins Stand.

Fitton Hill founder, Bill Greatorex (left), celebrates the club's first Standard Cup triumph in 1985.

*The 1985 Standard Cup final was a close run thing
with Shaw being denied by a single point (9-8) but
there was some consolation for stand-off Graham
Robinson (left) who took off the Ben Powell trophy.
Also pictured (above) is Shaw captain Barry
Gordon receiving the runners-up Berry Shield.
Both presentations are being made by the Mayor of
Oldham, councillor Kevin Leyden.*

Four random images from the match against Castleford on October 20th 1985.
Result: Oldham 46 Castleford 22.

Oldham pose to celebrate their new sponsorship deal with Seddon Atkinson in December 1985.
Back Row: M. Graham, D. Hobbs, D. Finch, M. Taylor, C. Hawkyard, M. Parrish.
Middle Row: F. Myler (manager), I. Sanderson, D. Foy, T. Flanagan, H. M'Barki, G. Warnecke, M. Worrall, B. Gartland (coach).
Front Row: K. Broadbent, P. Kirwan, R. Ashton, G. Woodhead (M.D. Seddons), D. Topliss, H. Ashworth, D. Liddiard, R. Ogden, M. Morgan, F. Howarth.

David Liddiard

Mal Graham

Gary Warnecke

Three of Oldham's more successful imports from "Down Under" in the 1980s in action at Watersheddings.
All three arrived for the 1985-86 season.
Full-back Liddiard was probably as fast as any player in the club's history.
Second-row forward Graham was a clever ball handler and play-maker who was given the captaincy.
Utility player Warnecke had a work rate second to none.

Challenge Cup quarter final action:
Above: Ray Ashton, Ian Sanderson and Mick Morgan watch with
interest as Terry Flanagan prepares to pass to Glen Liddiard in
the cup tie against Bradford Northern on March 16th 1986.

Left: David Liddiard sprints clear of Roger Simpson to score the
only try of the match.

Result: Oldham 6 Bradford N. 1.

A conversion that will live long in the memory of all the Oldham supporters lucky enough to be there. Mick Burke sends over the last minute winner following Paddy Kirwan's try against Wigan in the Challenge Cup 1st round on February 4th 1987.
The attendance of 10,050 was the last time a five figure crowd assembled at Watersheddings.
Result: Oldham 10 Wigan 8.

Mick Burke leaves the Runcorn defenders in his wake with Charlie McAlister in support on Easter Monday, 1988.

TOUR REPRESENTATIVES

Scrum-half, Mike Ford (left), and prop-forward, Hugh Waddell, were selected for the 1988 tour despite the fact of Oldham being in the second division. Promotion was achieved that season with both players being prominent throughout.

Aerial view of the Watersheddings site taken in January 1989.

Two action photos of Paul Round taking on Wigan's Steve Hampson in the match at Watersheddings on March 27th 1989. Other players are Mike Ford and Trevor Croston in the top image and Mike Ford, Keith Newton and John Henderson in the image below. Result: Oldham 21 Wigan 27.

Alan Davies turns back the clock and attempts a conversion in and amongst a group of ex-players, including a no doubt very interested Bernard Ganley (third from right), on the occasion of the centenary celebrations of the opening of Watersheddings on October 1st 1989.

1989

Right: Gary Hyde and Shaun Allen force a Rovers attacker to lose the ball.

Below: John Fieldhouse, Shaun Allen and Mike Ford give chase in the match against Hull K.R. on October 1st 1989. Result: Oldham 12 Hull K.R. 4.

The two clubs would conclude the season by participating in the second division premiership play-off final at Old Trafford, when Oldham turned a 29 - 6 deficit into a remarkable one point victory.

A late try from substitute Tommy Martyn sealed the win to leave the final score 30 - 29 in favour of the Roughyeds.

The week after Oldham had won at Widnes in the quarter-final of the Challenge Cup and queues form at Watersheddings prior to the match against Huddersfield on March 4th 1990. The added incentive of a voucher for a Wembley ticket boosted the attendance to 5,615 with the kick off being delayed by fifteen minutes. However, the Wembley dream went the way of all the others with a defeat to Warrington in the semi-final.

A super action shot of Paul Lord scoring one of his hat-trick of tries to the delight of the Oldham supporters in the 32 – 8 defeat of Ryedale-York on May 6th 1990.
This was the second division Premiership semi-final before Oldham went on to win the title against Hull K.R. at Old Trafford.

Spend £92,000, or RL ground shuts

ESTIMATED cost of work to be carried out to bring ground up to the safety certificate standard.

	COST £
POLICE CONTROL BOX	5,000
FULL ELECTRICAL CHECK OUT	2,000
STEWARD TRAINING	1,000
STRUCTURAL COST	2,000
MAINTENANCE REPORT	1,000
ANNUAL INSPECTION REPORT	1,000
CRUSH BARRIERS TEST	2,000
NEW TANNOY	5,000
NEW EMERGENCY LIGHTING	2,000
HUTCHINS STAND	5,000
WATERSHEDDINGS STAND	20,000
CLOSE CIRCUIT TV MONITORS	5,000
HERBERT STREET	30,000
GENERAL	6,000
DETENTION ROOM & EQUIPMENT	2,000
FIRST-AID ROOM & EQUIPMENT	3,000
FLOODLIGHT REPAIRS	2,000
	94,000

by ROGER HALSTEAD

OLDHAM Rugby League Club must spend £92,000 on ground-safety improvements next summer.

Failure to do so will mean closure of the ground.

The shock was revealed today by a club director, Mr. Tom Patterson, who has set up a meeting with local planning and safety officials for tomorrow to see what can be done.

CONDITION

Oldham has received a safety certificate which enables the Watersheddings ground, first opened 100 years ago, to stay in use for the remainder of this season.

But Mr. Patterson said: "A condition for renewal of the certificate for the 1990-1 season is that we must carry out essential safety repairs which will cost a figure approaching £100,000.

"I must stress that this is a safety matter — dealt with locally — and has no direct connection with the latest proposals in the Taylor report

TOM PATTERSON
. . . *meeting.*

An ominous pointer to the future!
The Oldham Chronicle highlights the vast amount of work needed to bring Watersheddings up to scratch for the 1990s.

Dave Cassells of Saddleworth Rangers made his tenth appearance in the Standard Cup final in 1991, an individual record, Dave helped Rangers to a 26 – 14 victory over St Annes.
His other final appearances were:
1976-78-80-81-83-87-88-89-90.

OLDHAM

GREYHOUND STADIUM

Licensed under the Betting & Lotteries Act, 1934
by the Metropolitan Borough Council of Oldham

OFFICIAL PROGRAMME **£1.50**

Tuesday 30th April 1991

Registered Office:
Oldham Stadium, Watersheddings
Telephone: 061-624 1343
Stadium Manager: Tim Wilby

Tote Manager: Alan Bates   *Accountant:* Barbara Lawrence
Handicapper: Stewart Leach

In April 1991 the greyhound track was taken over by the rugby club and the newly formed Oldham Greyhound Stadium Limited was to be managed by ex rugby league player Tim Wilby.
Here we see work being done to improve the facilities and the programme for the opening meeting under the new regime.

The start of a glittering career! Barrie McDermott crosses for his first professional try on his home debut against Leigh on September 1st 1991, John Henderson follows up in the background.
Result: Oldham 46 Leigh 19.

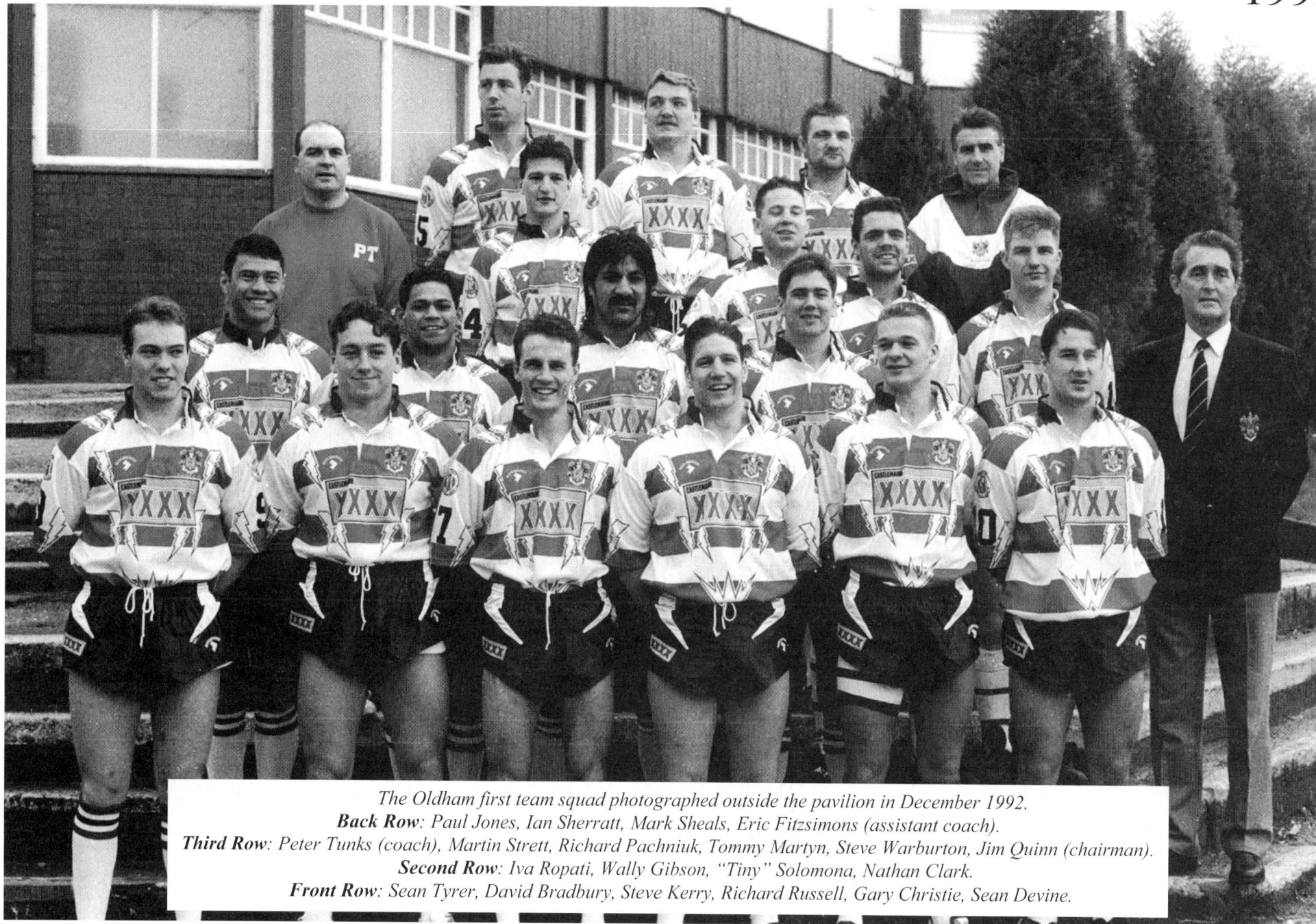

The Oldham first team squad photographed outside the pavilion in December 1992.
Back Row: *Paul Jones, Ian Sherratt, Mark Sheals, Eric Fitzsimons (assistant coach).*
Third Row: *Peter Tunks (coach), Martin Strett, Richard Pachniuk, Tommy Martyn, Steve Warburton, Jim Quinn (chairman).*
Second Row: *Iva Ropati, Wally Gibson, "Tiny" Solomona, Nathan Clark.*
Front Row: *Sean Tyrer, David Bradbury, Steve Kerry, Richard Russell, Gary Christie, Sean Devine.*

Flashpoint 1: The players of Oldham and Bramley sort out their differences on January 6th 1993.

Flashpoint 2: Two months later and this time it's Featherstone getting to grips with the Roughyeds on March 14th.

1993

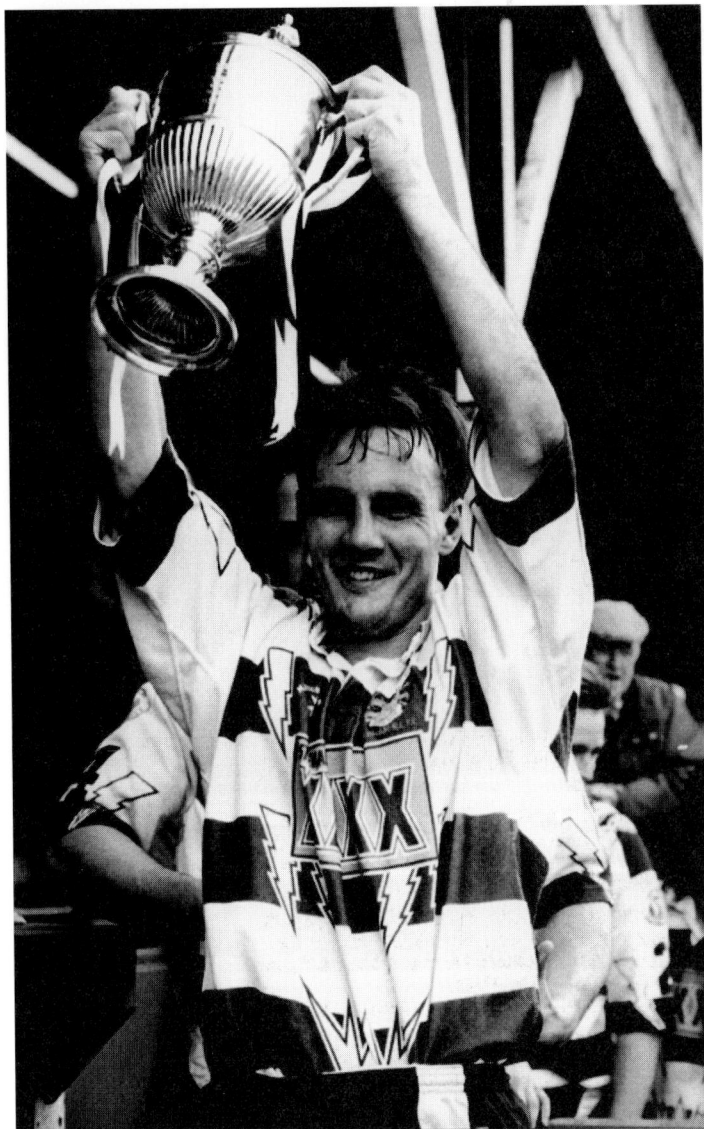

After the fixture was axed in 1981, the Law Cup was reintroduced and what was the fiftieth encounter took place at Watersheddings on August 22nd 1993.

Above: Oldham triumphed thanks to a last minute try from Martin Holden (much to the delight of long time fan Dave Blackburn).

Winning captain, Steve Kerry is pictured after receiving the cup.

Also shown is a table of all the Infirmary / Law Cup games played at Watersheddings.

DATE	RESULT	WON	CROWD
13- 5-21	WON	12-2	7000
9- 9 -22	WON	12-8	10000
13 -9-24	WON	15-4	8000
21- 8-26	WON	34-0	14000
13-10-28	WON	18-0	10000
25--8-30	WON	14-7	5000
27--9-32	WON	24-3	4000
18--8-34	WON	20-7	5996
22--8-36	WON	12-4	5000
20--8-38	WON	18-8	3000
16--8-47	LOST	17-18	8000
12--8-50	WON	10-9	5359
16--8-52	WON	25-8	11653
7--8-54	DRAW	17-17	7000
11--8-56	WON	34-5	8167
8--8-59	WON	28-11	10871
12--8-61	WON	53-13	6872
17--8-63	WON	29-13	5541
14--8-65	LOST	14-19	3937
12--8-72	WON	18-16	2060
17--8-74	WON	27-15	1365
15--8-76	DRAW	21-21	2016
6--8-78	WON	26-8	1301
3--8-80	WON	32-15	1622
22--8-93	WON	28-26	1360

Sale of land is good news for club as grant application is booted out

Watersheddings

COUNCIL BAIL OUT ROUGHYEDS

THE COUNCIL have come to the rescue of debt ridden Oldham RLFC easing their mounting cash crisis

Deeply in the red and having to make cutbacks in staffing, the future looked far from certain for the 'Sheddings outfit.

But Oldham Council have promised to buy 2.5 acres of land by the greyhound stadium.

Their plan is to sell this land, most probably for housing, with any profit put into the club.

Although neither party will reveal how much cash is involved council leader Cllr John Battye said it would go some way to easing the problems but they'd still have a sizeable debt.

Now the aim is to sell the land as quickly as possible. "We'd hope to move things fairly quickly because we'll run up interest charges if we're not careful," said Cllr Battye.

But he did admit this was a Godsend to the club: "They certainly needed help quickly and they've had to pay their creditors up which doesn't help.

"They are doing a good job though and if they can get through their present difficulties there's no reason why we shouldn't support a successful rugby club."

Oldham RLFC chairman Jim Quinn welcomed it but warned: "There's a long long road to furrow yet. This whole thing will take four or five years to address and that will depend on whether the club stays in the first division."

But it's not all been good news. On Sunday club directors were given the shattering news the Sports Foundation had turned down their bid for funding to redevelop Watersheddings.

The news left Mr Quinn stunned. In the past the Foundation have supported professional clubs looking for funding but they've now decided to withdraw all support.

Press reports from November 1993.

Over the next few pages there are a number of press headlines with varying degrees of hope and despair regarding the prospects for Watersheddings.

WATERSHEDDINGS, the home of Oldham Rugby League Club, may have seen better days but, for the club's supporters, it will always harbour unique and vivid memories.

Ever since Oldham moved to the ground in 1889, the tales of great players and great matches have inevitably mounted in number, in many cases becoming local legend, rather than stories based on starker, more realistic fact.

Now, though, Watersheddings, the birthplace of those often-told tales, seems unlikely to survive for very much longer and may even be bulldozed by the year 2000.

Outline plans were passed earlier this year to build housing on the 14-acre site, after Oldham Council and a property developer put together a rescue package for the debt-ridden club.

At the time, Oldham was £1.4 million in the red and, although the debt has since been cut to £200,000, the chances of the "Roughyeds" remaining at their spiritual home look slim, to say the least.

It is all a far cry from the club's halcyon days in the 1920s and 1950s, when Watersheddings was packed at every home game.

Now, crowd figures rarely rise above 4,000 and, although the team is re-establishing itself among the best in the league, a move to a new ground in Chadderton or Westwood seems almost inevitable.

Next to the rugby ground is Oldham greyhound stadium, the former base of Oldham Cricket Club which, as part of the council's deal, could be consigned to the same fate as its neighbour.

The track — opened 60 years ago and still attracting plenty of regular punters — was given a stay of execution earlier this year when a new 12-month contract was agreed for racing to continue there.

Some of the Watersheddings sports facilities have already disappeared, with a housing development, visible to the left of the greyhound track, replacing the rugby training ground.

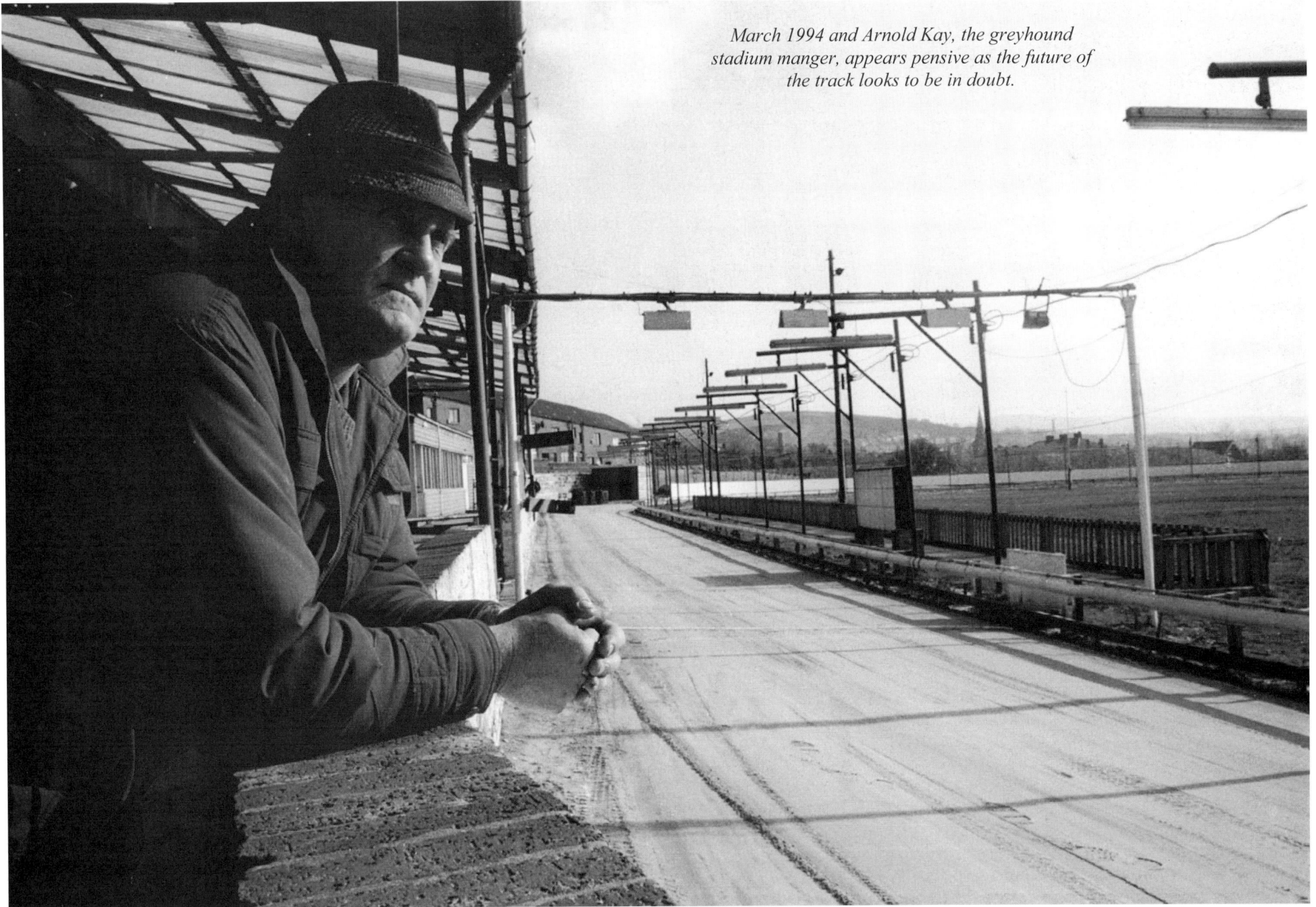

March 1994 and Arnold Kay, the greyhound stadium manger, appears pensive as the future of the track looks to be in doubt.

The under 19s Academy team in April 1994.

Back Row: *Alan Robinson (coach), Richard Badby, Michael Twist, Adie Meade, Mike Prescott, Anthony Crook, Stephen Hunt, Lee Bradbury, Simon Silcock, Damian Munro, Jodie Moran, Andy Smart, Geoff Munro (coach), Jack Buckley (manager).*

Front Row: *John Hollows, Wayne Ryding, Darren Hayes, Carl Parker, Alan Walsh, Neil Cartwright, Martin Breslin, Martin Halkyard.*

1994

Back Row— Paul Vincent, club solicitor, and Tom Patterson, club director.

Front Row—Keith Coates, Oldham Council Director of Economic Development; Jim Quinn; Oldham Rugby League club chairman, and Councillor John Battye.

EVERY PICTURE TELLS A STORY - OR DOES IT?

May 1994 — Contracts are signed on the pitch for the "historic" transfer of the Watersheddings ground from Oldham Rugby League Club to Oldham Council and the property group Brookhouse. The agreement was for the rugby club to stay at Watersheddings for a further three seasons, before moving into a council-owned stadium. The greyhound track was to remain open for a further twelve months, before making way for a housing development.

1994

The Chronicle headline from May 17th gives real hope for the Oldham supporters.

INSET :
Front page again two days later on May 19th 1994.

EVENING CHRONICLE

No. 33,543　　　OLDHAM, TUESDAY, MAY 17, 1994　　　Price 26p

Safe at last! Rugby deal secures future

'Historic' transfer at rugby stadium

THE transfer of the Watersheddings ground, from Oldham Rugby League Club to Oldham Council and property group Brookhouse Ltd, was completed today.

As contracts were exchanged on the pitch, rugby club chairman Jim Quinn said: "This is an historic occasion. The council's intervention has avoided the need to put the club in the hands of the administrator.

"Major creditors were paid off yesterday. The £1.25 million council rescue package did not clear all our debts, but most have been paid now and the remainder will be settled within a year.

"The club can hold its head up high for meeting this problem head-on and paying its debts, instead of putting the club in the hands of the administrator and walking away from it."

A winding-up order, involving several parties, was withdrawn in the courts on Monday.

Among major debts cleared off at a stroke were those to the bank, the Inland Revenue and Customs and Excise, totalling around £900,000.

The rugby club will stay at Watersheddings for three more seasons, before moving into a new, council-owned stadium, but the greyhound track will close in 12 months to make way for housing development.

Pictured (at the back) are: Paul Vincent, club solicitor; Tom Patterson, director. Front: Keith Coates, Director of Economic Development; Jim Quinn, Oldham RL Club chairman; and Councillor John Battye.

THE future of Oldham Rugby League Club is safe.

A £1¼ million rescue deal has finally been clinched to mark a new dawn for the cash-strapped club.

It will wipe away almost all the club's debts and give the team a plush new home.

The Watersheddings ground has been taken over by Oldham Council and developer Brookhouse Ltd, who have set up a joint company.

It has bought the greyhound stadium site and two residential properties owned by the club for £300,000 and has also agreed a three-year sponsorship deal of £425,000 and a £500,000 loan to the club.

The Watersheddings ground will continue to be played on for the next three years while a new stadium is built. It is then expected to make way for a housing development.

The formal exchange of contracts between the club and Oldham Council will take place on Thursday, after a winding-up order was rescinded yesterday.

The chairman of the rugby club, Jim Quinn, admitted: "The club would have been in the hands of the administrator by now, but for the council. Never again must anyone from Oldham Rugby League Club criticise Oldham Council for not helping it.

"We can now almost unload all our debt, which has been a major burden, and with that out of the way, we will hopefully be in a position to attract income from increased sponsorship, season-ticket sales, another share issue and one or two new directors.

"Income will be used to build a team which will be good enough to stay in the First Division permanently."

Mr Keith Coates, Director of Economic Development with Oldham Council, said that the exchange of contracts on Thursday comes after months of negotiation.

"Although it is not possible to be specific with regard to the location or design of a new stadium, it is our intention that the stadium will be ready by the beginning of the 1997-8 season."

He said the new rugby stadium would cater for other sports and leisure pursuits.

Stadium go-ahead tackles money problems

JIM QUINN: Aim now is a team to stay permanently in the First Division

377

1994

Watersheddings update by Roger Halst

Oldham keep the home fires burning

Old ground may

win a reprieve

OLDHAM should know within the next six weeks where their new stadium will be sited . . . and it might still be at Watersheddings.

Club chairman Jim Quinn gave nothing away when he told more than 140 fans at the club's annual dinner that negotiations with Oldham Council were at an advanced stage.

A decision about the new site was likely to be announced by Christmas, he said.

PUSH FOR GRANTS

Top-table guests at the fund-raising dinner included Councillor John Battye, leader of the council, and Councillor Jim Greenwood, chairman of the Leisure Services Committee.

A site at Boundary Park and another off Broadway are the most likely options, but don't rule out the possibility of Oldham continuing to play at Watersheddings in a council-owned stadium redeveloped by grants from national sources.

WATERSHEDDINGS — not dead yet

Council in rethink on rugby club future

Celebrations for victory in Super League

All-systems-go on plan to build a new rugby stadium in borough

by ROGER HALSTEAD

CLUB officials, supporters and civic leaders were today celebrating Oldham Rugby League Club's inclusion in the new £87-million Super League.

It was full-steam-ahead for the club, which will receive £900,000 a year for the next five years as part of media tycoon Rupert Murdoch's backing, and all-systems-go for the town in its plan to build a new stadium at Westwood.

Said club chairman Jim Quinn: "We have had a lot of adversity in the past few years, but this is terrific news.

"A lot of credit must go to Oldham Council, which has supported us magnificently in the past two years or so.

"Our shareholders and supporters have also played a major part in the Rugby League's decision to come up with a new Super League strategy.

"Three years ago we were stuck in a cul-de-sac. Last year we were staring at a large black hole, but thanks to Oldham Council, Rugby League in the town can now look ahead to a new dawn."

Councillor John Battye, leader of Oldham Council, revealed that the new stadium should be in use for the summer season of 1997. In that event, Oldham would have only one more full season at Watersheddings — 1996 — in addition to the short season to start in September, 1995.

The start of the Rugby League Centenary season in 1995 and club captain Martin Crompton and full-back Wally Gibson are pictured with mascot Sam Kershaw.

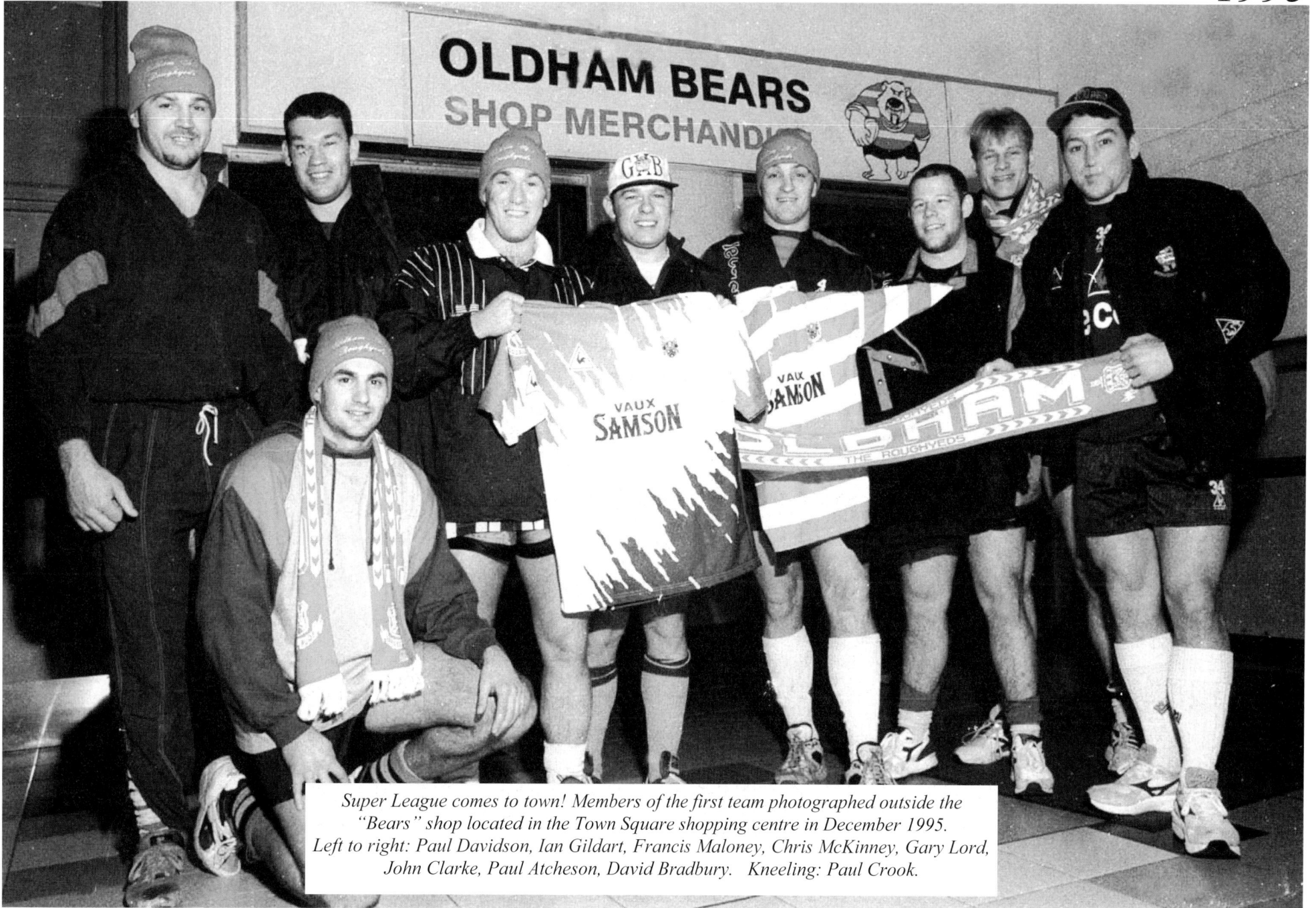

*Super League comes to town! Members of the first team photographed outside the
"Bears" shop located in the Town Square shopping centre in December 1995.
Left to right: Paul Davidson, Ian Gildart, Francis Maloney, Chris McKinney, Gary Lord,
John Clarke, Paul Atcheson, David Bradbury. Kneeling: Paul Crook.*

Martin Crompton, followed by Gary Lord and David Bradbury, leads out the Oldham team for the match against Sheffield Eagles on January 26th 1996.
This was the last match of the Centenary season and the last at Watersheddings before the Super League era.
Result: Oldham 26 Sheffield E. 16.

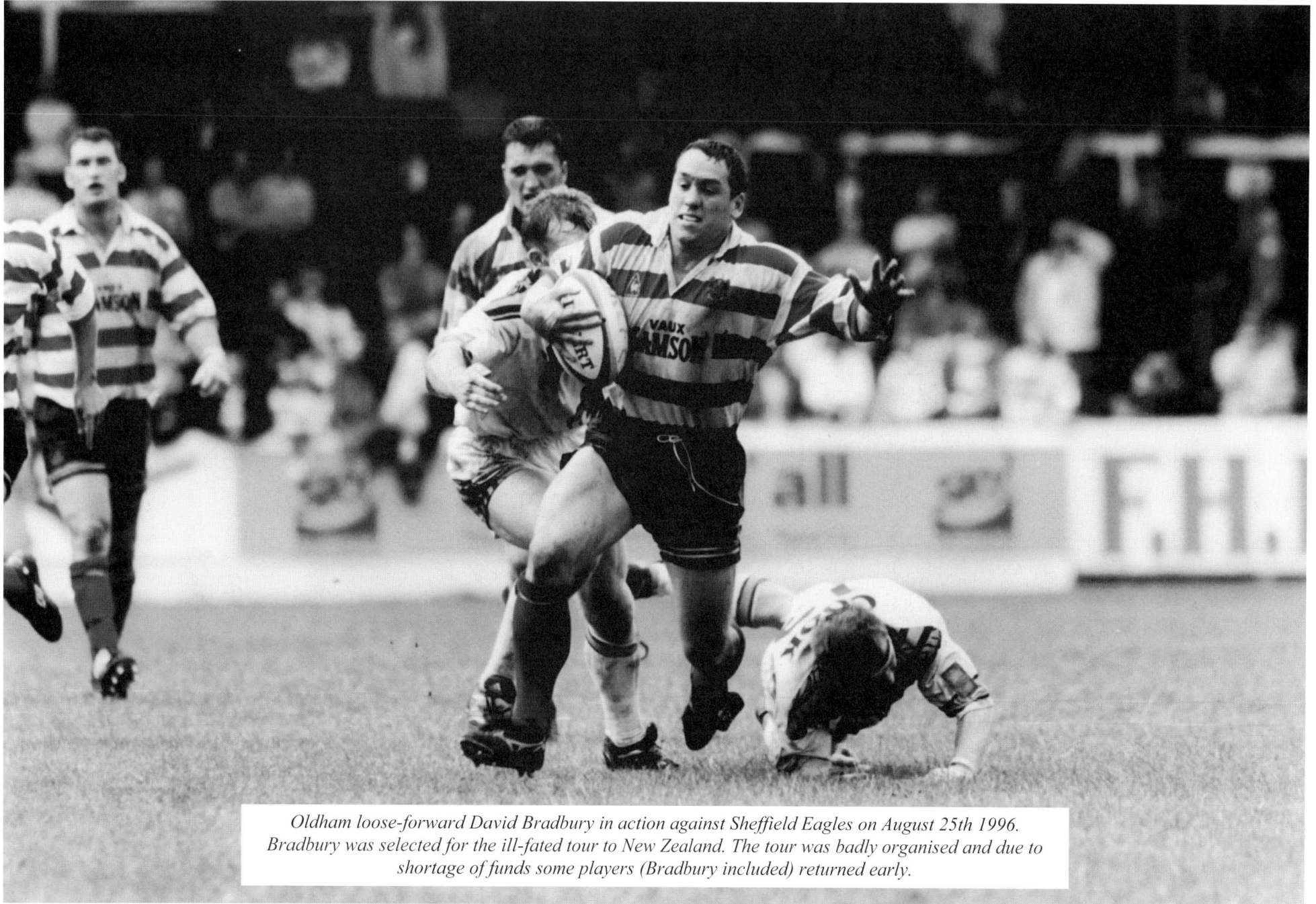

*Oldham loose-forward David Bradbury in action against Sheffield Eagles on August 25th 1996.
Bradbury was selected for the ill-fated tour to New Zealand. The tour was badly organised and due to
shortage of funds some players (Bradbury included) returned early.*

1996

The last Watersheddings recipient of the Ben Powell trophy was Saddleworth's Colin Garratt.

THE LAST STANDARD CUP FINAL AT WATERSHEDDINGS
Ninety two years after Heyside defeated Rochdale Rangers, John Fleming of Saddleworth Rangers becomes the last winning captain to lift the Standard Cup at Watersheddings after a hard-fought 22 – 12 victory over Higginshaw in 1996.
***Back Row**: Mick Worrall (coach), Anthony Brown, Peter Gallagher, James Wallace, Sean Whitehead, Gerrard Guilfoyle, Andy Proctor, John Fleming (captain), Nick Clough.*
***Front Row**: Emerson Jackman, Jason Wilkes, Chris Garforth, Danny Wilkins, Paul Coates, Paul Lord, Danny Tyrell, Chris Eaves, Colin Garratt.*

Higginshaw Standard Cup final runners-up 1996.

Back row: *A. Howarth, T. Millett, D. Atherton, S. Howe, C. Platt, C. Dickinson, A. Atherton, A. Whittaker, S. Butterworth, S. Lax, M. Coates (coach), J. Mellor (physio.), P. Whalley (sec.).*

Front row: *S. Quinn, D. Ashton, N. Lyons, M. Porteous, Jessica Mellor (mascot), K. Brennan, P. Ferris, A. Miller, J. Rogers, K. Tighe, R. Hadfield.*

The players make their way back to the pavilion after the match against Warrington in the first Super League season.

End of season awards at the conclusion of the first Super League campaign in September 1996.
Left to right: Paul Deacon, Joe McNicholas, Jim Quinn (chairman), Martin Crompton, Joe Faimalo, David Bradbury, Chris McKinney.

OLDHAM GREYHOUND STADIUM

LAST WATERSHEDDINGS MEETING COMMEMORATIVE PROGRAMME

1934 – 1996

Track and Handicap Manager: Mr J. Kay   Tote Manager: Mr M. Townsend
Racing Steward: L. Goodwin JNR

Official Programme   £1.50
Sunday 31st March 1996

SERIAL No. 242

The gates closed for the final time at the\Oldham Greyhound Stadium after sixty three years of racing on the track.

Putting on a brave face!
Oldham supporters at the last match against Swinton.

The Oldham and Swinton teams line up before the last official match at Watersheddings on January 19th 1997.

THE LAST DAYS!
The Ground.

1997

THE LAST DAYS!
Views inside and
outside the
pavilion.

THE LAST DAYS!
Players' Notices.

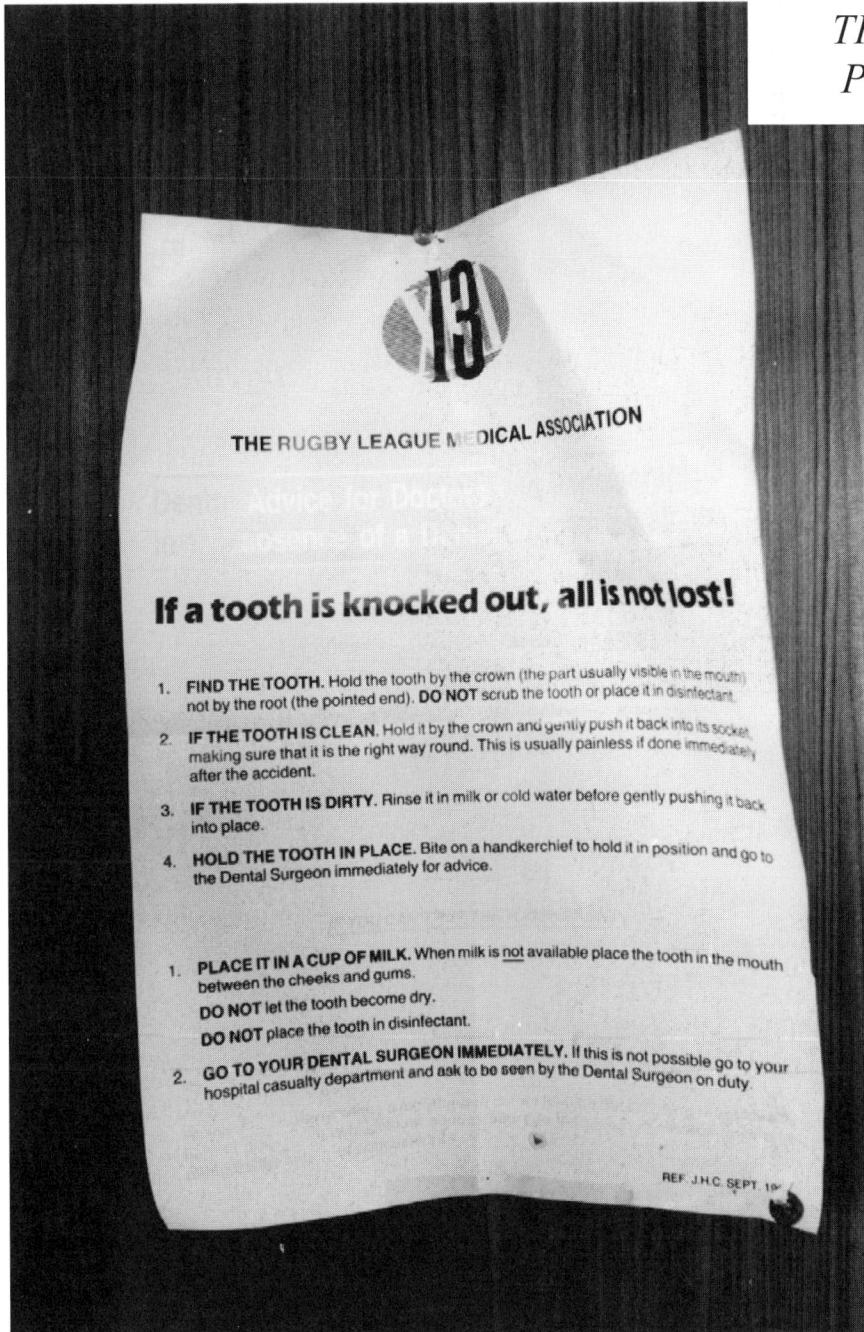

THE RUGBY LEAGUE MEDICAL ASSOCIATION

If a tooth is knocked out, all is not lost!

1. **FIND THE TOOTH.** Hold the tooth by the crown (the part usually visible in the mouth) not by the root (the pointed end). **DO NOT** scrub the tooth or place it in disinfectant.

2. **IF THE TOOTH IS CLEAN.** Hold it by the crown and gently push it back into its socket, making sure that it is the right way round. This is usually painless if done immediately after the accident.

3. **IF THE TOOTH IS DIRTY.** Rinse it in milk or cold water before gently pushing it back into place.

4. **HOLD THE TOOTH IN PLACE.** Bite on a handkerchief to hold it in position and go to the Dental Surgeon immediately for advice.

1. **PLACE IT IN A CUP OF MILK.** When milk is not available place the tooth in the mouth between the cheeks and gums.
   DO NOT let the tooth become dry.
   DO NOT place the tooth in disinfectant.

2. **GO TO YOUR DENTAL SURGEON IMMEDIATELY.** If this is not possible go to your hospital casualty department and ask to be seen by the Dental Surgeon on duty.

REF. J.H.C. SEPT. 19

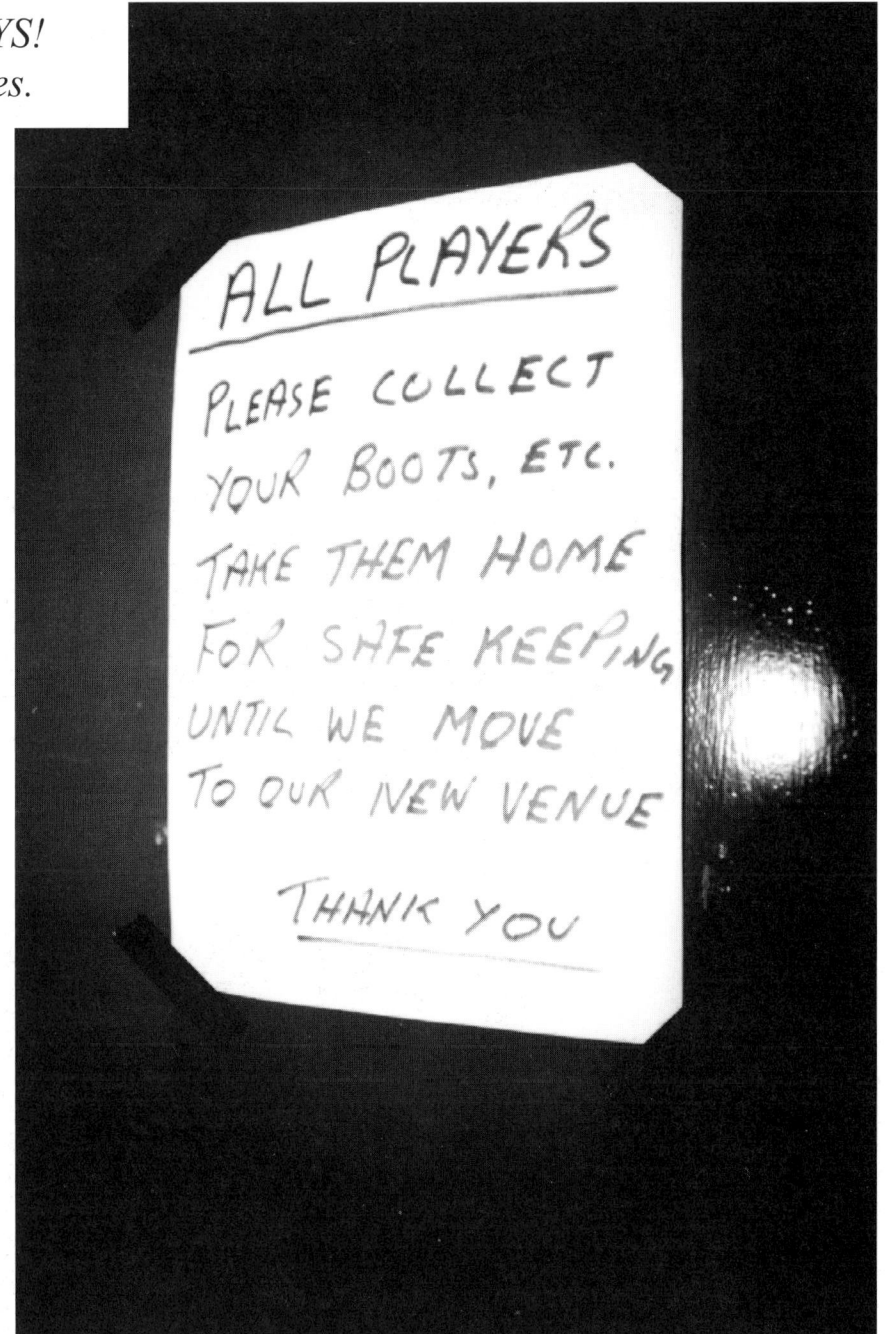

ALL PLAYERS

PLEASE COLLECT YOUR BOOTS, ETC. TAKE THEM HOME FOR SAFE KEEPING UNTIL WE MOVE TO OUR NEW VENUE

THANK YOU

1997

THE LAST DAYS!
The Pavilion.

HEARTBREAK!
A view of the Herbert Street terraces reduced to rubble during the demolition.
The site was sold off for a housing development but at least some of the legendary figures of the club were recognised when the thoroughfares were named.
So it is that Ferguson Way, Givvons Fold, Hutchins Lane, Jackson Mews and Winslade Close will provide a lasting reminder to the illustrious rugby past of the area which holds so many Watersheddings Memories. (Inset: Charlie Winslade's grand-daughters, Charlotte and Jaynee, photographed on Winslade Close.)

WATERSHEDDINGS MEMORIES

A collection of reminiscences - The supporters.

Watersheddings Memories... As a kid standing outside the pavilion cheering the players as they came out, especially Davies and Winslade. Then I would rush into the Watersheddings stand to watch the match. I liked Davies jinking in and out, proper centre play. Winslade barging down the middle. Half-time pie and coffee under the scoreboard then full-time rush back to the pavilion to clap the players off. Then run home with a smile on my face. We won!
Keith Shaw - Shaw, Oldham.

THE TACKLE!: A sunny Saturday, a packed crowd at 'sheddings, the visitors Wigan - Eric Ashton, Billy Boston, et al. A break-away by Ashton, a slipped pass to Boston and the giant is away. Only Ganley to beat. Our Bernard the best goal kicker in the world but not the best tackler! Billy decided he would score under the posts and Ganley would either move or be trampled. Bernard had only one weapon in his armoury "his backside". Just as Boston hit him, he half turned, Boston hit his backside, flew up into the air and half the Oldham pack pounced. Did we laugh!!!
Trevor H. Jones - Torquay, Devon.

I can thank my dad for taking me to Watersheddings in 1957 and having forty years of great memories. Hope for the same at Whitebank.
Barrie Gallagher - Scouthead, Oldham.

I was the mascot for the 1992-93 season and never missed a match home or away!
My mum would put red and white ribbons in my hair for all the home matches before I went to wait for the players in the tunnel. I can remember the old scoreboard with the team names hand painted in their club colours and that Mr. Laughton, who was later one of my teachers, was always up in the stand doing the video commentary. It always seemed to be cold at Watersheddings, one of the joys of winter rugby!
Jennifer Turner – Yasu City, Shiga Prefecture, Japan.

I remember being at a cup-tie against Wigan in the Watersheddings stand and it was packed to the rafters, so much so that, not being the tallest of people I could not see hardly any of the play. In fact the only time I saw the ball was when it was kicked high in the air. Eventually I decided enough was enough and I fought my way to the exit and asked the gateman to let me out. "You must be joking," was the reply. "If I open that gate to let you out about another hundred will try to get in!"
Arthur Brown - Coldhurst, Oldham.

Many wonderful memories, like when we knocked Wigan out of the Challenge Cup in 1987. There was snow on the hills, Watersheddings was floodlit and 10,000 crammed in, it was electric. Wigan were the World Club Champions in 1987 and had won everything else with players like Goodway and Hanley. Oldham were magnificent that night. Two key moments: Flanagan's cheeky trip on Gregory in back play to stop a certain Wigan try, and Paddy Kirwan's wonderful late flop over the line that sent the Oldham fans delirious with delight. Watersheddings was a place where Oldham Rugby League lived and breathed.
Graham Richmond - Walsall, West Midlands.

Fred Truman once said to me, "rugby league without Watersheddings would be like a horror film without Boris Karloff". Well, I for one miss the old monster.
Peter Young (former Oldham R.L.F.C. official) - **Delph, Saddleworth.**

WATERSHEDDINGS MEMORIES

A collection of reminiscences - The players. (taken from the Roughyeds "End of an Era" brochure)

All those years on I remember arriving in Oldham in February 1952. It must have been 10 degrees below freezing that night and at Mumps' Bridge when I got off the 98 bus visibility was nil. I had never been to Oldham before and it looked like as if I would not see much of it on this trip! You will understand my relief when I found the Red Lion. I had been a pilot in the RAF not a navigator. The bar was heated my bedroom was not but I benefited from the loose interpretation of the licensing laws that applied in Oldham at the time. The generous hospitality of the people of Oldham impressed me on that first night and during my 10 years living and working in the town and playing at Watersheddings that generosity never changed. **Sid Little.**

Watersheddings was more than a rugby ground to me. Even though eleven years in the first team at Oldham would seem enough experience to most people, my affinity with the place goes deeper. Being a proud born and bred Oldhamer and following my dad Bill and brother Kevin into the league scene of Oldham meant that 'sheddings was a familiar place from early days. My first recollection of the massive pitch was at the Standard Cup final in 1966 when St Mary's beat Langworthy. Little did I know then just how much of my sport and life was to be centred on Watersheddings. **Terry Flanagan.**

From the age of nine I always dreamt of leading out an Oldham team from the pavilion, through the eagerly awaiting spectators, up the tunnel and out onto the playing field. I achieved this ambition many times during my playing days and I can honestly say that they have been amongst my proudest moments during my career. **Mike Ford.**

The day that I was signing the Oldham secretary Bert Summerscales took me to lunch, then on to Watersheddings. I knew right away this was what I wanted. My move to Oldham was the best I ever made. I made a lot of friends, and have some good memories. I wish I could do it all again.
Thanks to Oldham supporters – you were fantastic! **Frank Stirrup.**

One of my funniest moments was crash tackling an opposing winger in to a disabled driver's Reliant Robin parked in the pavilion corner. My happiest beating Bradford Northern in a Challenge Cup replay in front of an enormous 18,000 Watersheddings crowd and my proudest being appointed club captain whilst progressing to a club post war record of 461 first team appearances. The years at Watersheddings were fabulous and given the chance I'd do it all over again. **Martin Murphy.**

During the 1950s Watersheddings was my home for four seasons and I recall with excitement those spectacular games played in an arena were the spectators were so close to the pitch. People forget that back then we played at the top level, in well over 40 games per season whilst holding down a full time job!
The Oldham Evening Chronicle wrote at the time "Never have so few provided so much pleasure for so many". It was an honour to play in front of the Oldham spectators and in later years be nominated to the club's Hall of Fame. **John Etty.**

I'm sure I hold the "fastest sending off" record at Watersheddings. I was substitute in a pre-season charity game against Blackpool coming on to the field on the 20 minute mark. Within a minute and without touching the ball referee Billy Thompson had me down the tunnel for an early bath. At least the water was warm! The same season we played the Aussies at Watersheddings. I was picked to prop against Artie Beetson who I think got wind of it and cried off! On retiring as an Oldham player I returned many times either as player or coach with Saddleworth Rangers on Standard Cup duty or later as the coach of Swinton. **Ray Hicks.**

WATERSHEDDINGS MEMORIES
A family perspective.

It is so difficult to pick out single memories from over forty years of watching the team at Watersheddings. As a boy, I lived in Prestwich, though my father was from Oldham, and took me to watch my first game at Maine Rd. when we lost in the Championship Final to Warrington in May 1955. With regard to actual games at Watersheddings, we began as regulars in the 'Penny Rush', always making sure we got there early enough for me to stand at the front on my dad-constructed wooden mini-platform (so that a 7/8 year old me could see!). As I grew, though, we graduated to the terraces opposite the main stand - and one of the earliest clear memories from there is of the awful 8-20 loss to Hull in the 1958 top-four play-off game, after having thrashed them 43-9 less than three weeks earlier - 'typical Oldham', my long-suffering mother would almost certainly have said! Why is it that so many of the clearest memories are of disappointing defeats? It must be something deeply psychological! But I can still recall as if they were yesterday two narrow, shock, home defeats in the Challenge Cup to Workington, in 1962 and 1982! The loss to St.Helens in the 2nd round of the Cup in 1987 also stands out as an awful memory, especially as it followed only 10 days after the fantastic 10-8 win over Wigan, when pure chance resulted in my family standing right behind the posts where Paddy Kirwan scored his famous match-winning try! The game v Leigh in January, 1984 also remains vivid - though not for any reason other than Mr. Mean's quite ridiculous decision to abandon it because of 'fighting' - though we were losing at the time, and we did beat them when it was replayed two months later!

That same season's game v the touring Aussies also stands out, as a very happy memory even though we did lose, and two other easily recalled occasions were, inevitably, the Scott Ranson hat-trick in the final Super League match to be played at Watersheddings. But, in many ways, certainly from a personal family angle, my most outstanding memory from the Watersheddings era is of a Slalom Lager Div. 2 game in October, 1981, against Keighley! It was the first time when I tried a full wife-and-two-children trip to the hallowed stadium; we then went half-a-dozen more times that season, and by then the whole family was hooked. Many years of huge enjoyment followed, with the current outcome being 10 extra members of Rugby Oldham, five of them in California, plus one son who earns his living writing about the game! The actual match? We won 21-12, with messrs. Flanagan and Goodway among the try-scorers. Happy days indeed! **Ian Wilson Macclesfield.**

Watersheddings was indeed the venue for many happy days of my youth, as my dad says. His memory of that first match he took us to are rather different to mine however – I had forgotten to take my glasses so spent most of the game squinting blurrily at large rock-like shapes running (what seemed at the time) aimlessly around a muddy field. It was my first experience of a large crowd and first exposure to somewhat colourful language in strong Lancashire accents (I was a gentile Cheshire lass) so in my myopic state it was a somewhat surreal experience!

But Dad is also right saying we were eventually hooked. I have many, many memories of being soaked to the skin, being so cold I couldn't feel my feet – we were always terrace people and it was only in the direst of weather that Dad would allow us to take refuge in the penny rush. But I also remember the feel of sun baking down and melting our customary half time mars bar and that amazing rush of adrenaline as time ticked away with the prospect of a win. My family is a creature of habit, so we always stood in exactly the same place on the terraces every week (and felt very aggrieved on the rare occasions when some unsuspecting away fan, or newbie took our spot), and I spent so much time jumping up and down on that wall, banging my feet against it and leaning over and banging on the advertising hoardings when particularly excited or aggravated. I had an autograph book and sometimes hopped over the wall at the end of the game – I remember the day I got my most treasured scrawl – Wally Jones, my absolute favourite player of all time! I grew from girl to young lady on the terraces and have to admit that my view of attractiveness was formed from the wide-shouldered, well muscled, bent nosed, hulks that I watched every Sunday (although I always preferred Mick Parish to Mick Morgan!). And if I ever get a whiff of linament these days it can transport me back to the beginning of a match when my heroes burst out of the 'sheddings tunnel – happy days indeed. My only regret about 'sheddings was that when they were selling off the turnstiles my dad refused to go and get me one!   **Jude Lawrence – San Mateo, California. U.S.A.**

Dad and Jude have pretty much covered it, and congratulations to whoever had the terrific idea of getting these memories down on paper. I'll just throw in a mixed bag of others. Parking near the top of Sharples Hall Street and walking around the back of the Penny Rush to get in - for some reason I still remember clearly arriving for a Lancashire game that had been awarded to Oldham, with Ian Sanderson selected for the team, but was then called off because of fog. There was the odd midweek A-team game - Dad really did get us hooked - when we'd have to stand on the terrace at the other side of the dugouts, because the Penny Rush side was shut. That Wigan Cup win, and the Australia tour game, in a 1986-7 season that also included a Lancashire Cup final appearance at Knowsley Road - and ended with relegation - remains unforgettable. Colin Hawkyard's try against the Aussies, plus Terry Flanagan and Bruce Clark getting stuck into Phil Daley and Ben Elias in the fights, will probably be recalled in more detail elsewhere. I'll also throw in a home game against St Helens in which Hawkyard and Tom Naidole scored terrific first half tries to establish a 17-6 half-time lead, only for Saints to come back and win 18-17 thanks to some combination of Graham Liptrot's hooking skills and Geoff Berry's refereeing (we hardly had the ball). A happier memory is of a 24-12 win against Halifax on New Year's Day when the pitch was covered with snow and Andy Goodway scored the finest individual try I can remember - although as I write, Sam Tomkins has just scored one for Wigan that might run it close. I'll always be grateful to dad for dragging us to that Keighley game (and to mum for letting him!) **Andy Wilson – Manchester. (Rugby League correspondent for "The Guardian")**

WATERSHEDDINGS MEMORIES

From the press and commentary box. (taken from the Roughyeds "End of an Era" brochure)

Wembley it might not be and Twickenham it certainly isn't. But the decaying terraces, the sloping pitch, and the primitive tiny dressing rooms beneath the grandstand at Watersheddings evoke just as many memories. Especially of the weather. Watersheddings has always been marked on my calendar as a two sweater and flat cap job even in summer! **Ray French.**

Watersheddings for me has always been a place of pilgrimage, even on those awful days when it has taken an hour and half to travel the umpteen odd miles from Halifax to Oldham due to severe weather or traffic problems. What really used to impress me was the fact that the ground was covered on all four sides, had that funny double-decker stand and every available surface was decorated in red and white stripes. It was an absolute picture. I am an avid collector of rugby league photographs and have many images of packed out, golden, olden days at Watersheddings. Of course, physically they are black and white or sepia or simply fading away but in my mind's eye they are a riot of red and white. And always will be. **Robert Gate.**

Watersheddings. The very name breathes the words rugby league. I've often reassured myself with the thoughts that my own club Featherstone Rovers and others like Barrow, Swinton, Batley and, of course, Oldham could not be connected with any other sport. You just can't begin to imagine robust northern towns, full of grit, soot and Roughyeds being called Saffron Waldon or Bishops Stortford. In 1928 the Championship final was held at Watersheddings. It was contested between Swinton and Featherstone Rovers. In those days the Rovers were upstart newcomers to the big league, with a fearsome pack of coal mining forwards. My granddad and his uncle Oliver set off the day before to walk to Oldham along with hundreds of others who couldn't afford both ground admission and charabanc fare. On that day they came home with blisters and disappointment. Rovers lost. I like ritual. I also like to have little ambitions. I've always wanted to visit Gracelands in Memphis. I made it a few years ago. Since my first visit to Watersheddings as an eight year old holding on to a big colliers hand I've wanted to go upstairs in Oldham's famous double-decker stand. I never have. Now I never will. Some ambitions you don't achieve. **Ian Clayton.**

The town will never be the same again. Like cotton mills and Platt brothers, Watersheddings will be confined to the pages of local history. Those who feel its passing will have memories stretching back to the golden days of childhood . They will recall happy times spent on the terraces with loved ones who first introduced them to rugby league to the Oldham team… and to Watersheddings. They will have private memories of dads, mums, aunts and uncles… of great games and brilliant players, big crowds football specials, straw around the pitch in winter, flat caps and posters outside the ground telling potential readers that the national papers had their big-name writers at the match. Farewell old friend and thanks for the memories. **Roger Halstead.**

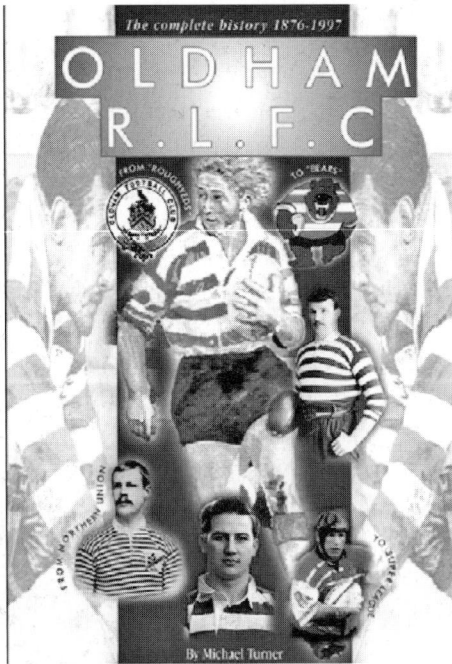

OTHER BOOKS PUBLISHED BY THE OLDHAM RUGBY LEAGUE HERITAGE TRUST.

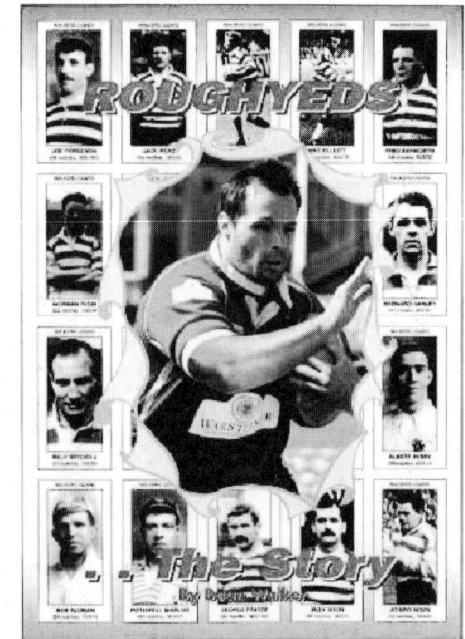

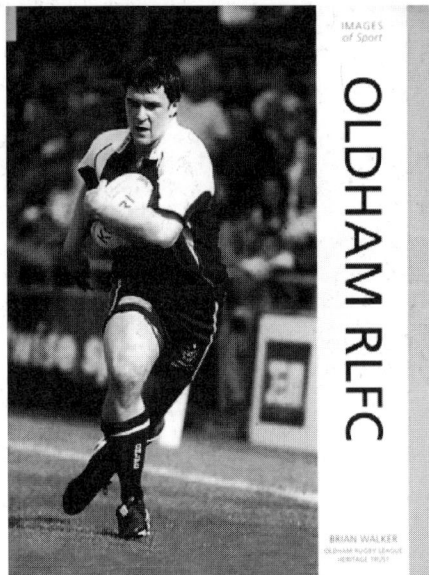

Top left:
Oldham R.L.F.C. The Complete History 1876 - 1997
Michael Turner.

Top right:
Roughyeds … The Story
Brian Walker.

Bottom left:
Oldham RLFC (Images of Sport)
Brian Walker.

Bottom right:
Kangaroos, Kiwis and Roughyeds
Michael Turner.

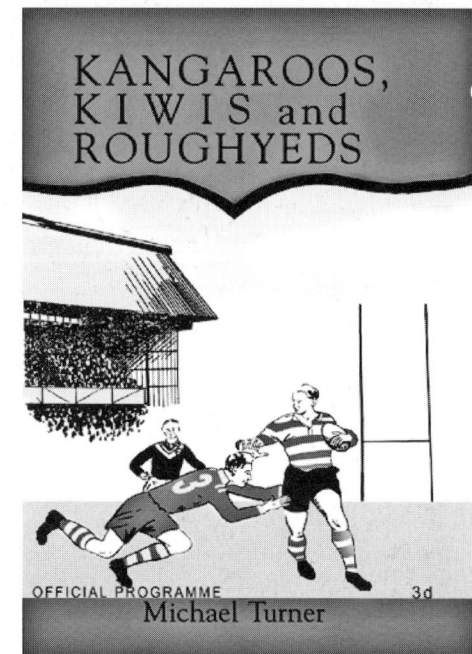